The
LITTLE
BIG BOOK
OF
WHITE
SPELLS

ILEANA
ABREV

ABOUT THE AUTHOR

Originally from Cuba, Ileana Abrev now lives in Queensland, Australia, where she has her own spiritual practice and conducts workshops on magic, spirituality, meditation, chakras, and crystals. She has built a reputation for herself as a respected white witch among her customers and clients. With knowledge passed down to her from her father, an esteemed Santero, Ileana guides customers on a daily basis to solve problems with magic spells and positive visualization. She has been a practicing witch for over ten years.

The LITTLE BIG BOOK OF WHITE SPELLS

ILEANA ABREV

Llewellyn Publications
Woodbury, Minnesota

This book was previously published as: *White Spells* (2001), *White Spells for Protection* (2007), *White Spells for Love* (2008), *White Spells on the Go* (2009)

FIRST EDITION
Third Printing, 2017

Book design: Donna Burch-Brown
Cover design: Kevin R. Brown

Llewellyn Publications is a registered trademark of Llewellyn Worldwide Ltd.

Library of Congress Cataloging-in-Publication Data (Pending)
ISBN: 978-0-7387-5169-6

Llewellyn Worldwide Ltd. does not participate in, endorse, or have any authority or responsibility concerning private business transactions between our authors and the public.

All mail addressed to the author is forwarded but the publisher cannot, unless specifically instructed by the author, give out an address or phone number.

Any Internet references contained in this work are current at publication time, but the publisher cannot guarantee that a specific location will continue to be maintained. Please refer to the publisher's website for links to authors' websites and other sources.

Llewellyn Publications
A Division of Llewellyn Worldwide Ltd.
2143 Wooddale Drive
Woodbury, MN 55125-2989
www.llewellyn.com

Printed in the United States of America

CONTENTS

WHITE SPELLS FOR PROTECTION

WHITE SPELL ON THE GO

WHITE
SPELLS

1
COLORFUL MAGIC

Each individual color in the spectrum gives out different vibration frequencies to our body and our everyday surroundings. Warm colors such as red and orange give out strong vibrations, while cool colors, like blues and pinks, give out passive vibrations.

We are light beings filled with colors known as the *aura*. Our aura changes according to the vibrations we give out. If you are stressed, you give out color signals associated with that stress to those around you. They know you are stressed not because you look scattered, tired, or are constantly having a bad-hair day, but they can feel the color signals you are giving out. If you haven't noticed by now, stress can be catchy. It is because unconsciously we absorb those color frequencies that are a big part of how we relate to one another.

A good example of this is when you are the last one to arrive for a meeting. The room is filled with people and immediately you feel uncomfortable; all eyes are on you. When you entered the room, the room was already filled with color energies blending and mixing together. Then here you come from having some type of an altercation with the person that took your parking spot. Due to this inner anger your aura has gone from a pleasant yellow to a bright red in a matter of a millisecond. And you ask yourself why 90 percent of the people in the room are looking at you. It's not because you think you still have the tag showing from the skirt you purchased for the meeting, but because of the color frequency you are giving out.

We know color is a part of our life. Then why not use color to aid us in our everyday living? When you are stressed, the last thing you need is a red dress to really enhance the stress levels. Maybe pick something with cool colors like light blues or pinks to keep the stress factor on a lower frequency. Now if you are depressed, the last thing you need are cool colors or black. This is when you need a bit of those warm colors like reds and oranges to strengthen the emotions and to lift the cloud hanging above you.

We all experiment with color from time to time in the way we dress, the way we decorate our home, the color car we have, or even the clothes we dress our children in. You will see a change in your children's learning skills if they were to wear yellow, which is a learning color, and green, which is a growth color. The potential would be endless for them. Now if you chose to dress them in bright colors like red or neon red, you are asking for a day filled with mischief. It's like a sugar high to a child.

Healing illness with color works much in the same way. If you have a chronic condition you need to cool it, not heat it. If you wish to heal an ongoing illness, blue is the color to use. It gives out cool healing energies that are also protective.

Color in magic has its advantages and should be used at all times when conducting spells. Candle-burning rituals, such as the ones in chapter 5, are a very good way to use color when directing an intent to the universe to manifest. It reaches the universe by the way we portray our needs and wants.

The universal color for money is green, so naturally you will use green for your prosperity and money needs. Love has been associated with pink, like a young, innocent woman's blush when she speaks to the man she likes. Her aura turns into a bright healthy pink as it's filled with love and hope to have her love returned in the same way. In the following chapters you will be using color to enhance your needs and wants to the fullest.

Below is a list of colors and their meanings. Use this guide to help enhance the power of any of the spells in this book. Add color to your wardrobe to enhance your needs and wants. Carry a colored cotton cloth with you at all times to manifest the dreams you wish to come true or to change your aura's frequency.

AMBER	Develops psychic skills
	Enhances your sexual drive
	For communicating with spirits
	For a deeper meditative state

BLACK	Wards off negativity
	Removes hexes
	Protects against evil workings
	For truth in magical workings
BLUE	Brings tranquillity to the soul
	Banishes anger
	Heals the body and the self
	For focus and relaxation before meditation
	Protects against others
GOLD	Strengthens the mind
	For intuition
	For communicating with angels on the higher realm
	For money spells
GREEN	Brings luck in business endeavors
	Attracts money
	Aids spiritual growth
	Heals the emotions
	Good for children

INDIGO	Useful when working with karma
	For meditation
	For psychic workings
LAVENDER	For spiritual development
	Works against stress in the home and at work
	Calms growing cancer cells
	Helps bring peaceful sleep
ORANGE	Promotes encouragement
PINK	Attracts friendships
	Brings love into your life
	To honor the self
	For communication between the self and spirit
	For self-love
RED	Enhances power
	For strength to fight against the odds
	For sexual passion and a passion for life
	Enhances sexuality
	Relieves depression

WHITE	Purifies the soul
	For working with spiritual guides
	Protects against dark workings
	Brings justice
YELLOW	Promotes learning in the young and old
	Sparks intuition
	Brings understanding when working with karma
	For happiness in life

2
CRYSTAL MAGIC

You work in harmony with the laws of nature when you work with magic, and crystals can be used as powerful magical tools. Crystals are minerals found all over the world. Ancient civilizations used them for healing and the art of magic. They also offered them to their deities to receive spiritual insight and guidance.

Crystals hold universal and Earth-bound energies that interact with an individual's energy to perform their magic. Each stone will feel different to each of us. For some people crystals feel warm; to others, cool. Some may feel a strong tingly sensation run up their arm when they hold a crystal, or perhaps a little lightheaded. Nearly all of us will find some type of inner peace when we hold one. We feel calm and relaxed because we have just made a bond with universal energies.

I believe crystals pick us. We can stand in front of hundreds of crystals of all different colors, shapes, and sizes and we will notice the one crystal that calls out, "Take me home!" It's as though this crystal knows your wants and needs, and with it you can manifest your deepest desires.

Crystals can be bought from New Age stores or any lapidary club or outlet. When you purchase a crystal, you must cleanse it when you get it home. Hundreds of people may have handled it, imbuing it with their own energies. It's important for you to cleanse it for your own well-being. There is no right or wrong way to cleanse a crystal. A small ritual I do to cleanse my crystals follows.

CRYSTAL-CLEANSING SPELL

On a full moon night, take your crystal out into the yard and gently place it on top of the grass. Look up and see the moon shine on your crystal. Visualize a silver light from above penetrate your crystal's heart and see little silver flashes of light now inside the crystal on the grass.

Rub both hands together and pick up the crystal. Hold it in your hands and visualize the needs you wish the crystal will help and aid you with. Carry it with you at all times and do not let anyone touch it as it belongs to you and the moonlight.

In the following crystal spells I assume the crystals have already been cleansed unless noted otherwise. Where I specify using other materials such as lavender water or salt to cleanse your crystals, you can use the above ritual as a guide or make up a cleansing ritual of your own.

Spells are like rites of passage. They help you to focus on your needs and desires so they can in turn be manifested. The most vital ingredients for your spells are emotion, feeling, and love. If you are true to yourself and others, magic will never do you wrong.

CRYSTAL SPELLS
FOR A GROWING PUPPY

Around the neck of your new best friend hang an amethyst heart to keep him or her from wrecking the house and backyard. (Note: Take care not to hang anything around a puppy's neck that he or she could get loose and chew or get caught on and choke.)

TO HELP YOU REACH YOUR GOALS

Fill a bowl with rainwater and add a hematite crystal to it. Leave it in a place where it will not be disturbed for three days and three nights. On the fourth day, hold the crystal in your hand and visualize the goals you are reaching out for in life. See them manifest in your mind's eye, then simply wait until they do.

MONEY MAGIC

In a clear, attractive bowl empty two cups of sesame seeds. Deep within the seeds hide a citrine crystal and a red jasper crystal. Place the bowl on your dining room table, and every month on the same date replace with fresh sesame seeds, keeping the crystal covered. Sit back and watch your money tree grow little by little.

WHEN DEALING WITH A LEGAL MATTER SPELL

Place a bloodstone crystal in a bowl, add the petals of seven marigold flowers, then fill it to the top with water. Hold the bowl up high and say, *"Oh, petals of the sun, give this crystal strength to fight.*" On the day of your legal hearing, take the crystal out and either hold it in your hand or put it in a pocket close to your heart.

FERTILITY MAGIC

Place a small pumpkin under your bed. Cleanse a carnelian pendant necklace by placing it out in the sun for an entire day. Place the necklace on top of the pumpkin every night before you go to bed. Then every morning hang it around your neck and pick up the pumpkin and rub it around your navel and pelvic area. As you do this, visualize your desire to be a mother and see yourself breast-feeding your wanted baby.

This ritual should be done every day for three months. At the end of that time, take the pumpkin to a garden filled with flowers and leave it there. Wear your necklace at every hour, including during sleep.

WHEN YOU'VE LOST A LOVED ONE SPELL

Bring an amethyst crystal close to your heart. It will remind you of the love, joy, and laughter you shared with your loved one. The crystal will help to heal the loss.

TO ATTRACT LOVE

On a piece of parchment paper write the characteristics of the person you wish to attract (do not use a name). Cleanse a rose quartz crystal with three drops of rose oil. Wrap the piece of parchment paper around the crystal and tie a pink ribbon around it. Bury the bundle under a rose bush on a Thursday at the stroke of midnight and say, *"Oh, Mother Earth, I give thee the person I wish to attract. May only beauty and goodness be seen in me by the person you hold deep within."*

Dig up your crystal on Friday at the stroke of midnight and leave a seed of a flower behind. Carry the crystal and its bundle with you at all times, especially when you are near the person you wish to attract.

TO ENHANCE SEXUAL DRIVE

Place carnelian in a white bowl with water. Add a teaspoon of salt and leave it outside for three days and three nights. When the time is up, hold the crystal close to your heart, visualize your desires and needs, and imagine making passionate love by the sea with the one you love so deeply. Keep the crystal in a red cloth bag and leave it under your pillow.

FOR A LOVED ONE NOT NEAR

Cleanse a crystal geode that has been sliced in half in a bowl of salt water (water with one teaspoon of salt added) once during the day and again at night for three days. Keep one half and send the other to your loved one. No matter what the distance, you will always be together.

FOR A LOVER

Place a tiger's-eye crystal in enough fresh rose petals to cover the crystal and leave it in a very special place for three days. When the time is up, hold the crystal tight and visualize your love penetrating it like a lightning flash. Give the crystal to the one you love with this thought in mind.

STAY FAITHFUL TO YOUR LOVER SPELL

Take a lodestone crystal to a tree with a bird's nest in it. Rub the crystal on the tree and say, *"Faithful I shall be like the birds nesting in this tree."* Take the crystal to bed and place it under the sheets where the pillow lies.

UNCOVER YOUR TRUE FEELINGS SPELL

In a bowl full of water add three drops of rose oil, the petals of a single rose, and a sodalite crystal. Leave for three days. After the third day, remove the crystal and keep it close to your heart. It will help you to uncover your true feelings.

RID ANGER AT SELF AND OTHERS SPELL

Bury a blue lace agate crystal deep in the roots of a lavender bush. Leave it for seven days and dig it up on the eighth day after 3:00 P.M. Hold the crystal in your hand, bring it close to your heart, and say, *"Blue lace agate with your calming blue, open my heart and take my anger so I may not direct it at myself nor another."* Wrap the crystal in a blue cloth and always carry it with you.

PROTECTION AGAINST AN ENEMY SPELL

Place seven rusty nails and seven black peppercorns in a clear bowl. Fill it with water and add a pinch of salt. Place a clear quartz crystal, a tiger's-eye crystal, and an Apache tear crystal in the bowl. Mix everything together, visualize protection from the one that wishes you harm, and say, *"Stay away my enemy, do me wrong no more."* Let the bowl sit for twenty-four hours, then place the crystals in a little blue drawstring bag and carry them with you at all times.

WHISK AWAY FEAR SPELL

Leave an aquamarine crystal in the sun for three hours. When it is warm, hold it in your hands and visualize heat entering your head. Think of nothing but the heat of the sun. The fear will subside and the crystal will give you strength to face each day.

PROTECTION FOR THE HOUSE SPELL

Leave four clear quartz crystal points outside your house on the night of a full moon. Pick them up the next day, hold them tight in your hands, and visualize protection for your home. Place the crystals inside your house, one at each of the four corners with the point facing toward the outside (i.e., toward the back or front yard). As you place each crystal say, *"With this crystal I protect my home from negative energies and bad entities."*

STRESS-RELEASING SPELL

Place seven amethyst crystals in a tall glass of water. Cover with a paper towel and leave outside for the night. Before the day starts, strain everything through a fine sieve or cheesecloth and drink the water. You will feel calm and totally purified.

FOR STUDY AND EXAMS

Obtain a citrine crystal and a fluorite crystal and place them in a white bowl. Fill the bowl with water and add a teaspoon of salt and three drops of rosemary oil. Leave it outside for three days and three nights. On the fourth day, hold the crystals in your hands and visualize excellent grades. Keep the crystals with you at all times when studying or taking exams.

TO FIND EMPLOYMENT

In a bowl of water drop a red jasper crystal, three cinnamon sticks, and a teaspoon of sugar. Leave this in a private place where the moon can shine on it for three nights and four days. Then hold the crystal in your hands and visualize the work you wish to find. Carry the crystal close to your heart at all times.

FOR DREAM RECALL

Cleanse a smoky quartz crystal in lavender water (water with two drops of lavender oil added) each night before you go to bed and then place it under your pillow. Keep a note pad and pen at arm's length. Write your dreams down as soon as you awake but before you get out of bed. As soon as your feet touch the floor, your dreams fade.

TO COMBAT INSOMNIA

Place two drops of pure lavender oil on an amethyst cluster. Hold it in your hands just before slumber. Visualize peaceful thoughts and happy dreams. Place the amethyst cluster in a purple sock under your pillow and go to sleep.

PEACE IN THE HOUSE SPELL

Place a rose quartz cluster in a large bowl and add water and three drops each of lavender and lemon oils. Let it sit for a day or so, then hold the bowl in your hands and visualize harmony and blissful peace. Place it in the room where arguments take place most often and you will soon experience harmony.

MAKE A WISH SPELL

Select a crystal that you are attracted to. Cleanse it with the cleansing ritual at the beginning of this chapter or with one of your own. Hold it in your nonwriting hand. Visualize your deepest desire, then see that desire penetrate the crystal. Take the crystal to a running stream and throw it as far as you can into the stream. As the crystal travels, your wish will follow.

3
BATH MAGIC

A bath connects us to the water element, and with the aid of herbs, crystals, and essential oils we can enhance its power. Having a bath nourishes the whole body, and the special properties of the herbs, crystals, and essential oils used can bring about a positive state of mind, as well as promote health and well-being.

Creating a magical bath with herbs, crystals, and essential oils can be further enhanced with positive visualization. This is when real magic is brought into the bathroom, encouraging relaxation and assisting in the manifestation of your dreams. When you get out of a bath enjoyed in this way, you will feel a lightness of being, as though you are walking on air. Your body will feel slightly tingly, and positive energy will be bouncing around you. The negative energy will spin down the drain when you let the water out.

The magical bath spells that follow use a lot of the old Santería ways and will inspire exploration and provoke laughter. In a magical bath it is important that you wet your hair. And the longer the bath, the better. No soaps or any kind of cosmetic detergents should be used. If you wish, have a full shower and wash your hair before you enjoy your magical bath.

After your bath but before the water is drained, collect everything you have put into the bath, and, if not specified in the spell, dispose of it anywhere except in the garbage bin. Finally, gently pat yourself dry after a magical bath to seal in the magic.

If you don't have a bathtub in your home, you may use the ingredients in a bucket filled with warm water. Then slowly let the water run from the top of your head to your toes.

BATH SPELLS
PROSPERITY SPELL

Draw a bath and to the water add a tablespoon of almond oil, half a cup of dried oats, ten seeds from a ripe tomato, and the petals from three tulips. Settle into the bath and visualize your wants and needs, imagining yourself manifesting them. After the bath, collect the tulips and oats, dry them in the sun, and then sprinkle them in front of a bank. Do this every Thursday for two months.

FOR MONEY

In a saucepan bring five cups of water to a boil. Add a handful of fresh parsley, basil, and mint leaves. Drain the herbs and keep the water for the bath. As you mix the herb water with the bath water, imagine money coming to you, and after you are in the bath, think only of financial security.

TO BRING ABUNDANCE

Add as much fresh basil, parsley, and alfalfa to a warm bath as you'd like. Also place the petals from a red flower in the bath for determination. Visualize abundance, see it happening in your mind's eye. When you least expect it, it will come.

TO ENHANCE PSYCHIC ABILITY

Add a bunch of fresh celery, one teaspoon each of dry saffron and thyme, five large bay leaves, a small bunch of honeysuckle, and two large cinnamon sticks to a bath. Visualize a rainbow of colors emerging from your third eye and getting larger and larger and connecting with the universe.

TO ATTRACT LOVE

Put three large cinnamon sticks, a bunch of fresh basil, seven cooking cloves, and six cups of water into a large pot. Place the pot on the stove and bring to a boil. Drain the herbs and empty the water into your bath. Add the petals of a pink flower, a daisy, and three pansies. (Note: Choose your flower carefully to avoid allergic reactions, harmful effects from oils, etc.) Sink in and feel the loving energy all around you. Imagine your aura changing to a loving, passionate red. Repeat this spell for three consecutive days, beginning on a Friday, the love day.

FOR LUCK

Add to your bath a cup of pineapple juice to sweeten any sour thoughts. Visualize everything working out just as planned.

TO ATTRACT WOMEN

Add five bay leaves and one teaspoon of crushed fresh ginger to your bath. Visualize as many women as you can, and imagine yourself embracing them. Do this on Tuesday because this is when Mars attracts. After the bath, collect the leaves and dry them in the sun. Carry them with you in a little red drawstring bag at all times.

TO ATTRACT MEN

Draw a bath and add one teaspoon of barley and the petals of three pink flowers. (Note: Choose your flowers carefully to avoid allergic reactions, harmful effects from oils, etc.) Sit in the bath and visualize the man you want in your life. Do this on Friday when Venus attracts.

BEFORE GOING OUT ON A DATE SPELL

Draw a warm bath while holding three red roses close to your heart. Petal by petal, drop the roses into the bath with thoughts of a possible new love. Add a teaspoon of dry damiana, gently sprinkling it in just before you bathe. In the bath, visualize your date and how you would like it to end.

PASSIONATE EVENING SPELL

One by one, place the petals of three red roses into a bath with three drops of basil essential oil to enhance a night of passion and love. When you are in the bath, visualize a flame burning bigger than the universe itself. When you get out, gently pat yourself dry, collect the petals, and dry them with a white tissue, pressing them down hard. Put the petals in a little red bag with a teaspoon of dry saffron and place it under your pillow.

FIND YOUR SOULMATE SPELL

Peel three apples. Add the peels to the bath together with one teaspoon each of dry barley and lemongrass to spice things up. Sit in the bath and visualize your soulmate. Do this for seven days, beginning on a Friday. After each bath gather the peels of the apples, dry them (but not in the sun), and keep them behind your front door.

BEFORE A BRIDE'S WEDDING DAY SPELL

In a bath add six drops of lavender essential oil and seven different colored flowers. (Note: Choose your flowers carefully to avoid allergic reactions, harmful effects from oils, etc.) Gently recline in the bath and relax.

FOR COLDS AND FLU

Collect a bunch of fresh eucalyptus leaves, break them in half with your hands, and place them into the bath with five drops of eucalyptus oil. While in the bath, imagine a clear, fresh forest and its pure refreshing scent.

AFTER AN ILLNESS SPELL

Draw a bath and in it add the petals from three white roses, three white gardenias, and three white carnations, with a sprinkle of dry rosemary. Do this on Sunday, the healing day.

CHEER THE SOUL SPELL

Slice an orange and a lemon in half and place them into a bath with three drops of neroli essential oil. Like the steam in the bathroom, imagine any heaviness of the heart slowly dissipating.

PURIFY THE SOUL SPELL

Draw a bath and to the water add the milk of one fresh coconut and the petals of a white flower. (Note: Choose your flower carefully to avoid allergic reactions, harmful effects from oils, etc.) Visualize yourself rising to the heavens, feeling free and full of love, with universal energies dancing all around you. You are connected and purified.

TO BREAK NEGATIVITY

Place half a cup of vinegar, a bunch of fresh rue, and a tablespoon of salt in your bath. (Note: Rue can cause dermatitis upon contact with skin.) Light a white and a blue candle close to the bathtub. Imagine yourself as pure light, with nothing entering you but pure universal energy. Visualize the negativity leaving every pore of your body.

ANGER-DISPELLING SPELL

Draw a bath and add five violets and their leaves and three drops of lavender essential oil. When you sit in the bath, remember that a word said in anger hurts not only yourself but others around you. It eats away at peaceful energy.

TO STOP GOSSIP

Add a fistful of cooking cloves and two teaspoons of dry blessed thistle to your bath. Visualize a barrier going up between you and the gossip to keep it at bay.

TO SETTLE CHILDREN FOR THE NIGHT

Give your children a bath with a few drops of lavender essential oil added to it. They will magically drift off to sleep.

DREAM AT NIGHT SPELL

Add seven jasmine flowers, a bunch of holly, and three drops of peppermint essential oil to your bath. Visualize yourself dreaming and enjoying your dream world. Enjoy this bath directly before retiring.

FEEL PROTECTED AND SECURE SPELL

Gather as many three-leaf clovers as you can (of the kind with white flowers that have not been recently sprayed with pesticide or herbicide), either at home or at the local park, making sure the stems are attached. Place the clovers in the bath with three sticks of chopped celery. Visualize yourself as a knight wearing a shining armor that protects your body and soul. Know that no one can penetrate your shield.

MAKE A WISH SPELL

Get two large sunflowers and drop them petal by petal into the bath with a fistful of crushed sage. (Note: Do not use sage if you are breast-feeding; it can dry up the mammaries.) Sink into the bath and visualize your wish up in the clouds, floating in the heavens and being nursed by loving hands. Imagine your wish materializing.

4
HERB AND
PLANT MAGIC

Herbs are one of the most important tools you can use for magic. For centuries, they have been used for their healing and magical properties. Today, our pharmaceutical medications are simply synthetic versions of what our ancestors used to use.

Like humans, plants connect to the four elements: air, water, earth, and fire. Without these elements, plants and humans could not possibly exist. We all need air to breathe, water to drink, earth to feed from, and fire for warmth and light. But at times we take our environment for granted. When was the last time you admired a wildflower in a field, or touched a mighty oak tree? This is something a lot of people don't get to do every day, and as a consequence they lose touch with nature. Remember, one of the most prominent colors in the world is green. It signifies growth, which brings understanding, courage, prosperity, and healing.

All herbs and plants grow above ground. From the smallest shrub to the tallest tree, they feed sacred spiritual energies from the womb of Mother Earth. Once dried they can be used for incense when burned on a charcoal tablet. The charcoal is placed in the middle of your censer and once lit it gives out a dark smoke. After the initial smoke disperses, the charcoal tablet becomes red hot. This is when you can add your magical incense.

Always remember, when picking leaves from a plant to do magic, cook, or when cutting flowers to give to a loved one, never pull it totally from its roots. Always ask permission from Mother Earth when clipping and leave a token as a form of payment or thank-you, like a crystal or a new seed of any kind.

Herbs can also be used as *amulets*. Amulets are charms or ornaments used for protection or for an intent. They can be seen in jewelry or carried in little bags which I refer to in this chapter as "drawstring bags." You can purchase these bags if you wish, or you can make your own with a piece of cotton material of the color specified for the particular spell you are doing and simply place the contents in the middle, make a bundle, and tie it at the top with some string. Following is a number of herbal amulets you can make to use at home or work, or for protection against the negativity that may seep into your everyday life.

HERBAL AMULETS
MONEY MAGIC

In a green bowl mix one teaspoon each of powdered ginger, Irish moss, and sesame seeds. Crush together to form a powder, and as you crush it visualize your money needs.

Light a charcoal tablet and on top add a quarter teaspoon of your money powder. Concentrate, breathing slowly and steadily. Do this for ten minutes every night for seven nights, beginning on a Thursday night just after the sun goes down.

FOR MONEY IN YOUR PURSE OR WALLET

If you find yourself without a cent, sprinkle dry sassafras in your purse or wallet and you will always have enough for the things you need to buy.

PROSPERITY SPELL

Sprinkle fresh alfalfa sprouts in the front and back of your house. As you do this, visualize your most wanted needs and recite the following: *"May the ground take this offering I give. May it bring me prosperity which is in great need."* Do this seven times every Thursday, and don't be shy—sprinkle plenty of alfalfa sprouts.

FEMALE FERTILITY SPELL

Find a bunch of fresh mistletoe and leave it indoors to dry until it becomes brittle. (Note: Mistletoe berries are poisonous; do not ingest.) Place the dry mistletoe inside a little orange drawstring bag. Carry it with you everywhere you go, and at night place it under your pillow. It will strengthen the female reproductive system.

MALE FERTILITY SPELL

If you want to enhance your fertility, eat lots of carrots, carrot seeds, and bananas in groups of threes. It will aid performance like never before, with sperm count levels way up.

TO FIND LOVE

Dry three apricot seeds. Make yourself a little pink drawstring bag and drop the seeds inside with three drops of ylang-ylang essential oil. Visualize positive thoughts of love in your life.

LOVE NOTE

Write a note to the one you love on a Friday evening, then gently rub a bunch of lavender buds on the notepaper. Blow the buds to the wind and say, *"May the fragrance of lavender carry my thoughts to the one I love."* When your love opens this note, nothing but your loving thoughts will matter.

TO ATTRACT WOMEN

In a little cup add three drops of sandalwood oil, two drops of cedarwood oil, and one bay leaf. Mix together and let stand one night under a full moon. As you set the cup on the grass say, *"Strength and magnetism this leaf shall have, no female will ever resist the male energy it has, attracted they will be to the male they see in me."* Carry the leaf every time you go out and you will attract lots of females.

TO ATTRACT MEN

In a little red drawstring bag insert a teaspoon of dried catnip and hang it around your neck. Like a cat that goes crazy when it smells the "magical scent," so, too, will men be attracted to your scent.

TO ENHANCE SEXUAL DRIVE IN MEN

In a little red drawstring bag insert three acorns, the top of a green banana, and three shells of oysters you had consumed and dried in the sun for three hours. Keep this close to your lower extremities (like in your pants pockets) and you will see a change for the better in your sex life.

TO ENHANCE SEXUAL DRIVE IN WOMEN

Get one dry typha leaf (better known as cattail) and while visualizing your sexual needs, place it in a little red drawstring bag. (Note: It is illegal to gather cattail in some areas.) Keep it with you at all times.

TO ATTRACT FRIENDS

Make yourself a little pink or purple drawstring bag. Let the peels of one lemon dry for three days. Then put the peels in your little bag and add a teaspoon of passionflower petals and a bloodstone crystal that has been cleansed with lavender essential oil. Hold this little bag in your hands and visualize yourself in a place full of people, talking, laughing, and having fun. Keep this little bag with you when you need a friend around.

PROTECTION FOR THE HOUSE SPELL

With a red ribbon, tie a bunch of garlic to the corner by your front door. It will protect you and your loved ones from negative vibes that may enter your house. Never let anyone use the garlic for anything else.

PROTECTION AGAINST INTRUDERS SPELL

Get a fresh, whole coconut, drain it, and cut it in half. In a bowl mix one teaspoon each of fresh rosemary and basil and half a cup of uncooked rice. Blend these together, then fill both halves of the coconut with the mixture. Fit the coconut together and wrap a white ribbon around it to keep it shut. Go outside on a Sunday night and bury it in the backyard. It will protect your home and backyard.

TO RID NEGATIVE FORCES FROM THE HOME

At the front and back doors of your house hang two bunches of clover upside down. As you hang each bunch, feel the negative energy around you and direct it to each bunch. The clover will then set out to fight the negativity around your house.

PROTECTION FROM EVIL SPELL

Make four little blue drawstring bags, each the same size. Mix in a bowl two teaspoons each of dry angelica, Solomon's seal, and balm of Gilead buds. (Note: Fresh angelica closely resembles poisonous hemlock which can be fatal.) As you do this, visualize your house protected from evil. Divide the mix into four equal amounts and fill each bag with it. Hang or hide the bags in the four corners of your house.

COURAGE SPELL

Sprinkle a pinch each of dry yarrow and thyme in your shoes. (Note: Yarrow can cause dermatitis upon contact with skin.) While you wear them, your fears will stop and you will have the courage to accomplish what you have set out to do. It will encourage self-worth and make you feel ten feet tall.

IMPROVE THE MIND SPELL

In a little yellow drawstring bag place three vanilla beans broken in half, a bunch of fresh rosemary, and the petals of a lily of the valley, and wear it around your neck. (Note: The leaves of lily of the valley can cause skin irritation.) With each breath visualize your mind becoming stronger, remembering dates you will not want to forget.

FOR A JOB INTERVIEW

In a jar big enough to fit a hand's full of crushed pecans, add three drops of rose oil, and keep a lucky hand (root of an orchid) inside with the lid shut tight. After three nights, place your lucky hand and the crushed pecans in a little red drawstring bag, and take it with you to job interviews. With this little bag you will feel confident while questions are being asked, and you will have a good chance of getting the job you want. Don't let anyone else see the red drawstring bag.

FOR THOSE WHO PLAY TO WIN

In a green bowl mix together one teaspoon each of poppy seeds, dry angelica, and dry chamomile. (Note: Fresh angelica closely resembles poisonous hemlock which can be fatal.) As you do this, visualize winning not only at cards, but at everything you do. Put the herbs in a little green drawstring bag and carry it with you at all times.

FOR SLEEPING PROBLEMS

Make yourself a little purple drawstring bag, and as you do this think of having a good night's sleep. Inside, add a teaspoon of dried valerian, and each night hold it in your hand while you lie in bed. Before you know it you will be soundly asleep, and when you awake, the little bag will be somewhere in your bed.

FOR SPIRITUAL AWARENESS AND PSYCHIC STRENGTH

In a medium-sized jar half-filled with almond oil add a teaspoon of dry yerba santa, damiana, and spearmint leaves, with seven drops of lime essential oil. (Note: Spearmint oil is toxic and the leaves can cause dermatitis.) Mix together with a plastic spoon and screw the lid on top. This is to be used before spiritual healings or for divination purposes. Place three drops on your hands before you start, rub them gently together, and place on your forehead. Then bring your hands to the back of your neck, breathe deeply, and start your work. You may even like to use this blend in your bath.

FOR ASTRAL TRAVELING

In a little purple drawstring bag place two teaspoons each of dry angelica and crushed peppermint leaves, and add a smoky quartz that has been cleansed with lavender essential oil. (Note: Fresh angelica closely resembles poisonous hemlock which can be fatal; also, peppermint oil is toxic and the leaves can cause dermatitis.) As you do this, visualize what you would like from the astral realm, and every night before you go to bed rub the drawstring bag on the bottom of your feet. This will take you where you want to go and protect you along the way.

5
CANDLE MAGIC

Candles are more than just decorative lighting for dinner parties and romantic evenings. The flame of a candle emits universal energy. It also brings light into our lives, not only so we can see in the dark, but for our spirit to communicate with the heavens.

The flame of a candle can be likened to the human spirit. No matter what the circumstances, we all have a living flame within. This flame dwindles at times when we lose hope and our future seems dark and uncertain. But we can rekindle the flame over and over again, and it will burn until our work here is done.

Humans have often used fire to pay homage to higher powers. It's now time to pay homage to ourselves, for in reality *we* are the higher power. We are the ones who can bring creation or destruction into our lives.

Candle-burning unites our spirit with the candle's flame. With visualization and concentration, a candle can act as a beacon, sending messages to the universe. When you visualize your desires, try to do it in a positive manner, and respect the destinies of others—they are not yours to change or play with.

Candle-burning can become complicated because of the different colored candles used. I have made this type of ritual as simple as possible, but there are things you must know before you start.

When partaking in the rituals that follow, you may want to find a special place where you will not be disturbed. You will need a medium-sized card table covered with a white or purple cloth. This will be your altar. You will also need candle holders and an oil burner that you may purchase at any outlet that carries aromatherapy oils and essences.

Your altar will always have two candles on it for the day of the week. The altar candles will change color depending on the ritual being done. In each ritual, I will tell you which colors you need.

In many spells I have not specified how long a spell should last; that depends on you and your time. Just remember that the more concentration and visualization you put into any of the spells, the better the outcome of your intent.

Use the list below as a general day-by-day guide. You can also use the candles for times when you want to enhance the specific attributes that the color of the candle represents. For example, if you want to nurture strength and passion, burn a red candle. You can burn it on any day of the week; it doesn't necessarily have to be on its designated day.

SUNDAY	Yellow to aid healing of the self and for learning something new.
MONDAY	White for purity and protection.
TUESDAY	Red for strength and passion.
WEDNESDAY	Purple for wisdom and family communication.
THURSDAY	Blue for patience and tranquillity.
FRIDAY	Green for love to grow in your life.
SATURDAY	Black to rid negativity from the week that has just passed, and to promote positivity for the week that is coming.

In a lot of the rituals you will need to use a candle of the color associated with a person's astrological sign, called an *astral candle.* For this, refer to the following list.

ARIES	March 21–April 19
	White
TAURUS	April 20–May 20
	Red
GEMINI	May 21–June 21
	Red
CANCER	June 22–July 21
	Green
LEO	July 22–August 22
	Red
VIRGO	August 23–September 22
	Black
LIBRA	September 23–October 22
	Black
SCORPIO	October 23–November 21
	Brown

SAGITTARIUS	November 22–December 21
	Gold
CAPRICORN	December 22–January 19
	Red
AQUARIUS	January 20–February 18
	Blue
PISCES	February 19–March 20
	White

Once you decide on a spell, purchase tapered, colored candles that burn the same color from beginning to end. The whole candle must be the color nominated, that is, don't use candles that are white inside.

The candle is divided into two parts. From the middle up toward the wick is called the *North Pole,* and from the middle down is known as the *South Pole.* Now that you know this, you can start to *dress* the candles before the ritual. To do this, search your kitchen for some olive oil, vegetable oil, wheat germ oil, almond oil, or coconut oil. Rub a small amount of oil in your hands, pick one candle up at a time, and with your right hand rub up toward the North Pole, and with your left hand rub down toward the South Pole. Never rub the candle in an up and down motion. As you do each candle, visualize your needs and wants and why you want to do the ritual.

Some of these spells may continue over a few days, but if it is not specified, you should finish the spell on the same day. There is no need to purchase more candles unless some of your candles burn quicker than others. If you do need to purchase another candle, dress it accordingly. Never blow a candle out for you will blow away the candle's energy. Instead, use a snuffer or your fingers.

Once you have finished your spell you may still have some candles left over. Never use these candles again for a new spell. You may use them around the house, but not for an intent. And whatever is left on your altar cloth, dust it to the wind.

Also, be aware of fire hazards. Never leave candles unattended or alone with children.

CANDLE-BURNING SPELLS
ATTAIN SUCCESS SPELL

Light two blue altar candles on a Thursday night, and burn three drops of lime essential oil in your oil burner. In a small bowl place some crushed nutmeg, and sit back and visualize your intentions for success.

Next, light your astral candle and around it light four orange candles. Sit or stand, and in your mind's eye see the success you wish to have. Every five minutes bring the orange candles closer to the astral candle. After the candles are grouped, spread out your arms, look up at the heavens, and finish the ritual by saying, *"Flame of these candles, I reach out to the universe for strength to bring me success. I need it now. My intentions are to harm no one, and this is the only way I wish to gain it."* Let all the candles burn to the very end and repeat when success is needed.

FOR MONEY

Light two blue altar candles on Thursday after dusk, and by the side of each place two bunches of fresh basil. Around each bunch of basil sprinkle poppy seeds, and imagine money walking through the front door in any shape or form.

Next, light your astral color candle in the middle of your altar table while still visualizing money. Then at each side of your astral candle light two green candles and say, *"Hear me, oh Divine, I'm calling thee. With these candles I send you my money needs. Find it here or there, I really don't care, but bring it to me so I may feed my money needs.*" Do this for fifteen minutes, then snuff the candles. Repeat for five consecutive days, and as you do this every day move the green candles a bit closer to your astral candle so that at the end of the five days the three candles are as close as they can be and are working on your money needs.

SUCCESSFUL BUSINESS SPELL

Light two blue altar candles on Thursday just before the full moon, visualizing your business and what it needs. Burn three drops of basil essential oil in your oil burner and light three frankincense tears (frankincense incense cones) on your censer to keep away negativity.

With your business still in mind, light five green candles if your business is open five days a week, six if open six days a week, and so on. Burn the candles every morning for thirty minutes for seven consecutive mornings, and watch your business grow. Repeat when things are slow or when you feel it needs another push.

FIND THE PERFECT MATE SPELL

Light two green candles on a Friday night. On a charcoal tablet add a pinch of dragon's blood powder (*Daemonorops draco;*

Dracaena) and a bit of crushed cinnamon stick. While you do this, visualize your perfect mate.

Next, light your astral candle in the middle of your altar. Light four pink candles around your astral candle, and make sure that you place one of each of the pink candles to face north, east, west, and south. In the middle, sprinkle petals from pink flowers, preferably roses, then say, *"I call all the corners of the world: north, east, west, and south. Hear me: I am looking for my mate, and I need your help to find him/her. Search for me, high and low, and I will be waiting with open arms for this person to come into my life."* Sit back and watch the candles burn in unison while the universe searches for your perfect mate. Let the candles burn right to the end.

TO BE ASKED BY YOUR LOVER
FOR YOUR HAND IN MARRIAGE

Light two red candles on a Tuesday night. Burn three drops of rose essential oil in your burner, and on top of your altar table scatter the petals from two red roses. While you are doing this, visualize the way in which you would like your lover to propose to you.

With this in mind, place your lover's astral candle in the middle of your altar and around it light three red and three pink candles alternatively in a circle. Say out loud, *"As these candles burn, so alight my desire to wed. [Name of lover] and I have been together for a long time. We have talked about marriage and now with this spell I hope to initiate a proposal. There is a mutual love and respect between us, so if it is to be, let love conquer all."* Sit back and relax while visualizing the wedding day you have always dreamed you would have. When you are ready, snuff the candles and repeat for three consecutive nights.

TO HEAL A MARRIAGE

Light two purple altar candles on Wednesday and tie a red ribbon around something you both shared that once brought you together in love and laughter. Place this item in the middle of your altar, and burn two drops of patchouli essential oil in an oil burner.

Next, light an astral candle for each of you, then light a red and an orange candle and place them on each side of your partner's astral candle while visualizing strength and love. See your marriage as it is and what you would like it to be. See yourselves talking and coming to an understanding about what has gone wrong and how you can heal it. Then say, *"I don't know if I deserve the loneliness I feel. I am willing to work to heal whatever is missing. Our love still burns like the flames of these candles. Oh, Divine, make my love's heart glow with happiness once again. Make me understand his/her sadness. By Lady Venus, I wish it be."* Relax and think of what you have just done. Snuff the candles. Do this ritual for three consecutive days, and always remember that communication is the key to a healthy marriage.

MEDITATION SPELL

Light two white altar candles on any day of the week. Burn three frankincense tears (frankincense incense cones) on a charcoal tablet, and for a little bit of inspiration add a pinch of crushed mandrake root on top. (Note: Mandrake root is poisonous; do not inhale.)

To open up your third eye, continue by lighting two purple candles. In the middle of them place a lapis lazuli crystal that has been cleansed with lavender essential oil. Start your meditation as usual, and repeat whenever you meditate.

TO CALM THE ANGER OF A LOVED ONE

Light two purple altar candles on a Wednesday in the name of the person you wish to calm down. Place a lotus root on your altar and visualize the tranquillity and peace you wish your loved one to have. (Note: It may be illegal to gather water lily [lotus] roots in some areas.) Burn three drops of lavender essential oil in your burner.

Next, light the person's astral candle, and with seven light-blue candles make a circle around it. As you burn the candles, bring this person to mind. See him or her being angry, then becoming less and less so until you can bring a smile to his or her face. Send out thoughts of peace and love, imagining tranquil seas or a mountain calm and strong. Snuff the candles. Do this ritual every Wednesday for as long as needed.

FIND LOVE WITHIN SPELL

Light two green altar candles on a Friday night, and as you do this visualize the love you wish to cultivate within—a love without reservations or hate. Bring to your altar a bunch of fresh pink flowers and have them displayed in a vase. Feel the freshness and beauty they bring. Smell them and feel the peace.

Next, light five pink candles in a circle, and in the middle place a rose quartz cluster that has been cleansed with salt water (water with one teaspoon of salt added). Under the cluster place a piece of paper with your name on it. Visualize the flames warming your heart and say, *"I am a good person, I love who I am. No longer will I feel anger or hate inside me, only gladness that comes from knowing and accepting who I am and what I will become."* Do this for about fifteen minutes, then snuff the candles. Repeat only on Friday for seven consecutive weeks.

FOR LUCK

Light two yellow altar candles on Sunday and burn three drops of vetiver essential oil in your oil burner. Sprinkle crushed nutmeg on your altar table and visualize bringing luck into your life.

Next, light a black candle and see all your bad luck being consumed with the flame. Then light two green candles for growth and hope, and see your luck changing. As you stand back, visualize your needs. Then lift your hands high and say, *"Let luck come into my life, and may it change it. I am a simple soul, searching and wondering if I am worthy of all my goals. I* mean no harm to others, I just want to get on with my life and leave behind all my bad luck." After ten minutes, extinguish the candles. Repeat every evening for three consecutive days.

OVERCOME AN ILLNESS SPELL

Light two yellow altar candles on Sunday and sprinkle crushed eucalyptus leaves on your altar table.

As you visualize yourself being healthy and on top of the world, light an orange candle. On each side of the orange candle light a red candle, then stand back, and watch the flames burn your illness away. Sense the strength within you to overcome your illness and say, "I will no longer thirst on weakness. My strength will help to heal me, and I will regain my health." Snuff the candles and repeat every Sunday until a change in health can be seen by you and others.

TO SEND HEALING ENERGIES
TO A SICK FRIEND OR FAMILY MEMBER

Light two yellow altar candles on Sunday. Crush a fistful each of dried calamus and peppermint leaves together until a powder is formed. On a charcoal tablet burn a quarter teaspoon of this powder while thinking of the person you would like to

58

send well-wishes to. On a piece of parchment paper write down the person's name and on top of it light his or her astral candle.

While still focused on the illness of your loved one, light four white candles and two red ones, and in front of them light a black one. With the black candle visualize the person's illness melting away, with the white candles visualize him or her healing, and see the red one giving him or her strength. Snuff the candles, and if you wish, do this ritual every Sunday until you see the person getting well, then repeat once a month to help keep up his or her courage and strength.

END AN ADDICTION SPELL

Light two red altar candles on a Tuesday night. In the middle of your altar place the addictive substance that you would like to give up (e.g., a cigarette, alcohol, or some type of drug). Cover your addictive substance with a black cloth and around it wrap a black ribbon. Visualize yourself despising it with an intensity only an addict can have.

With this in mind, light your astral candle and around it light seven red candles for courage and strength. Stand by your altar and bring to mind the pain, the hurt, the lies, and the abuse that an addiction can inflict. As the candles burn so will your desire for the addictive substance. Snuff the candles and repeat every day for seven consecutive days while you go cold turkey. You may do this ritual for a loved one too.

PROTECTION FROM EVIL SPELL

Light two black altar candles on a Saturday night, and crush one teaspoon each of blessed thistle and rue into a powder. Light a charcoal tablet and add the powder, but only a little at a time. Add two or three frankincense tears too (frankincense incense cones). While all this burns on your charcoal tablet, think of the evil you wish to be gone.

With this in mind, light two white candles to represent the purity and truth of your heart, and two red candles to give you strength and courage to fight the evil. Then light a black candle and feel the evil fade as the candle melts. As this is happening say, *"I'm stronger than the evil around me. I'm pure and white with nothing to hide. May good overthrow evil at every turn."* Let the candles burn for half an hour, then snuff them. Repeat for two consecutive nights.

FOR AN ENEMY TO BE GONE

Light two black altar candles on Saturday, and as you do this visualize the wrongs your enemy has inflicted on you. Burn three drops of frankincense essential oil in your oil burner to clear negativity, and on a piece of parchment paper write the following: *"Be gone my enemy [name of enemy]. Be gone and never set foot on my front door."*

Immediately light a black candle and place the parchment paper under it. Then light a pink candle and say, *"[Name of enemy], find love instead of hate; find peace and love within your soul. Let me be, and stay away from me and my loved ones."* Sit back and visualize your enemy walking happily away, leaving you alone once and for all. Snuff the candles and repeat every day for seven consecutive days.

CALM THE HOME ENVIRONMENT SPELL

Light two purple altar candles on a Wednesday and burn three drops of lavender essential oil in your oil burner. While you are setting this up, meditate on the household concerns that are stressing you out.

Next, light a blue, pink, and orange candle, and as you do this visualize peace, tranquillity, and harmony being established between you and the people you are living with. Step back and watch the flames burn, then say, *"Disharmony be gone, bring peace to this home."* Meditate for ten minutes on the love and peace your home needs, then snuff the candles. Repeat every night for a week.

TO SEEK HELP FROM YOUR GUIDE

Light two white altar candles on any day of the week. As you do this visualize your guide being around you and say, *"I need your guidance on this day."*

Once focused, place in the middle of the candles on the altar a vase full of fresh white flowers and say, *"These are for you for always being here for me."*

Fill a glass with water and place it on your altar table and say, *"This water is to bring you clarity and spiritual growth."*

Light two purple candles, then sit down and talk to your guide about what is troubling you. You will begin to feel a sense of peace that only your guide can bring, and before you know it you will have your answer. Visualize for as long as you wish, and repeat the ritual whenever you need advice or guidance from your spiritual guide again.

FOR STRESS

Light two white candles on any day of the week. Burn one drop of ylang-ylang and two drops of lavender essential oils together in your oil burner. Feel the peace around you as you relax and unwind for a few seconds.

Next, light two blue candles for peace and tranquillity, and between them place an amethyst cluster. Feel the energy of this crystal calm you.

Then, while still focusing on the peace and tranquillity that you greatly need, light an orange candle and see its color surround you and free the stress. Once finished, sit down, relax, and visualize all the stress leaving your body, going back to where it came. Let the candles burn right to the end. You may do this ritual as often as needed.

TO HELP YOUR CHILD
ON THE DAY OF AN EXAM

Light two yellow altar candles and burn three drops of rosemary essential oil in your oil burner. Visualize your child sitting down with the exam papers, ready to begin.

With only thoughts of your child in mind, light an orange candle to give him or her courage and concentration to go through with the exam. Then light a blue candle and visualize your child relaxed. Last, light two yellow candles to enhance his or her intellect. Stand back and look at all the candle flames for a few minutes. Visualize your child reading and writing without hesitation as the questions are answered carefully and knowingly. Let the candles burn until your child gets home, then snuff the candles. If you wish, conduct this ritual every time a test comes your child's way.

WHITE
SPELLS

☆ FOR ☆
LOVE

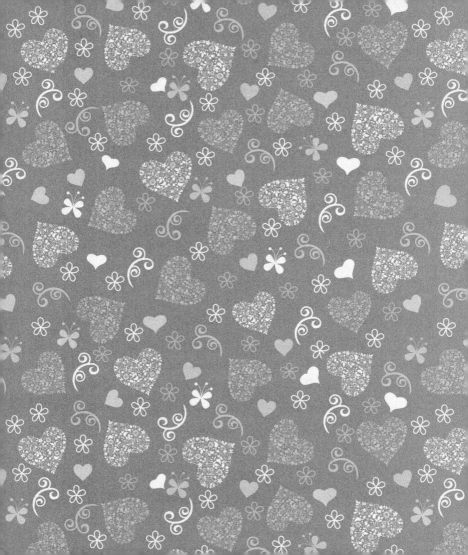

INTRODUCTION

LOVE AND MAGIC

I asked a few of my friends what love means to them, but apparently that question is more difficult to answer than I thought it would be. I had expected that everyone would know what love means to them, but none of my friends had a spontaneous answer for me, leaving me totally bemused. After my friends had time to give the question some thought, though, I did receive answers:

Love is to trust someone completely and to care about their well-being above your own. Love is devotion and independence, admiration and respect. Love is having someone who brings out the best in you. Love is a connection that makes you smile every time you see the other person. Love is a comfortable feeling of well-being and affection.

Love is a deep desire to protect the one you love. Love is friendship, honesty, happiness, affection, and sharing. Love is contentment, companionship, passion, and desire. Love is finding that missing piece that completes you. Love is friendship, kindness, and the little things that matter. Love is pure happiness. Love is the feeling that you don't want anything to change—ever! Love is when you find yourself mirrored in someone else. Love is everlasting and unconditional. Love is friendship, family, and children. Love is growing old together.

All of this is well and true, but what really *is* love? We keep asking ourselves this question over and over, and the only thing we know about love is that it feels no hate, it has no anger, and it sees no fault. Love is blind to defects and it speaks many languages. It sees no race or color except the color of the soul. Love brings happiness and laughter; it brings joy and enchantment. Love gives people strength, understanding, and courage—but most of all, love forgives and holds no hatred or malice.

When you first feel love, it's like a hidden trigger that activates unknowingly and automatically. "Why am I feeling this way?" you ask yourself when you experience the alien sensations—the weakness in your knees, the butterflies in the pit of your stomach. You aren't able to explain why you can't eat or drink, why you can't concentrate or make sense of your thoughts and feelings; you definitely can't explain your inner hunger to see the other person again. But if you have all of these symptoms, the diagnosis is simple: you're falling in love.

Some people say that love is nothing more than a heightened state of physical attraction, and it's true that being alone and feeling lonely can manifest feelings of love for another. Are you sure you're in love, or are you just lonely for companionship? This is a question you should ask yourself when you think you're in love—because if it's not real love, it won't be everlasting.

An elderly couple walking down the street holding hands is, to me, one of the most beautiful sights there is. If that isn't everlasting love, I don't know what is. Imagine everything that couple has gone through together: the ups and downs of life, the everyday little niggling, their first fight, their first child—not to mention grandchildren and declining health due to age. We all want this type of love; we want the friendship, the companionship, and the "in sickness and in health" bit. The problem is how to find love like that, how to keep it and hold it for the rest of your life.

That's the type of love I and others call romantic love. Romantic love has no gender limitations; it's the love associated with relationships, and it's invigorating, exciting, and emotionally exhausting. Romantic love can sometimes be hurtful, but it laughs because it holds no anger or resentment. The best thing about romantic love is that it can forgive over and over again wholeheartedly no matter how many times the same wrong was done by the one you love.

Romantic love can move mountains when it's appreciated, when it's treated with deep, unconditional affection and respect. It is responsible for the solid and durable happiness in our lives, and without romantic love we may feel we have no purpose. We can spend a lifetime trying to find a soul mate, vowing not to stop trying until we actually do find the romantic, everlasting love we've always wanted.

The older we get, the more we want romantic love, and the more we appreciate its endurance. Those who maintain that they don't want this enduring love are only kidding themselves. Everyone wants someone else in their life; it's part of human nature. We *need* love. We need to receive love and give love, but in order for us to exist in harmony with those around us, love must be given and received unconditionally. If we can accomplish this, the possibility that we'll live a full and meaningful loving life is endless.

I remember watching an old black-and-white movie when I was younger in which one of the male characters said to a woman: "You are beautiful because you are loved." That line of dialogue has stayed with me throughout my life—and the older I get, the more I appreciate the value of those words. "Beauty is in the eye of the beholder" may be an oft-used phrase, but that doesn't make it any less true. When you are blinded by the beauty within a person and not necessarily by their exterior facade, you love that person unconditionally without scrutinizing their looks, faults, or material circumstances.

People obviously also worry about money, their jobs, and their families, but I can honestly say that at least 75 percent of the people who come to see me for spiritual guidance do so because of issues relating to love—such as how to find it, keep it, and heal it. And they ask me: can I use magic to get it?

Magic is what dreams are made of. Magic is the air we breathe and the memories we cherish. It's an energy itching to manifest our innermost desires. Magic is the power of positive thinking. Magic can't be seen, but it can be felt, and that's what makes it mythical and mystical. Magic is the vessel that carries our wishes to the universe.

Why not project your desires of love to the universe and manifest the love you've always wanted? This can easily be achieved with positive visualization. Everyone consciously visualizes the unreachable and says, "I wish I could have that," projecting their needs and wants with positive visualizations designed to cause intentional changes, a direction of will to accomplish goals and desires. When these goals and desires do manifest, people call it magic, because what they had thought was impossible has now come to be. These manifestations are indeed magic at its best, and by adding items such as herbs, a few candles, or even crystals to your positive visualizations, you create magical spells.

A spell is the reinforcement of a positive visualization. In spells, objects with natural energies are used, such as candles, herbs, or crystals. Each of these objects represents and reinforces the art of positive magic, and they are what I call "the tools." Without these tools, a positive thought sent out to the universe is just a positive visualization.

The tools needed in conjunction with a spell keep you focused on the task at hand. For example, imagine that a dear friend has recently gone through a relationship break-up. You wish her strength to cope with her broken heart, and you decide to turn to magic to aid her pain. As you start to gather the tools needed for the spell, your mind is already focused on one thing—your friend! This focus reinforces your intent, and you begin to build an energy that can't be seen but is certainly felt and heard by the universe.

The universe is out there waiting for our wishes, and I can assure you these wishes do get seen to and are very much scrutinized. Remember that the universe is looking for sincerity in our spells, not just wants based on a whim. Love magic should not be used in any way to manipulate love. It distresses me to know there are people out there who will go to any length to manipulate love and who will stop at nothing to get it.

A few practice something very alarming, something I call *dark love*. I've been asked on numerous occasions to practice dark love on a person someone believes is their everlasting love. Unfortunately, those who come to me for this purpose don't listen to reason. They want results for something I know will only bring sadness—and at times misfortune—to the innocent, and karmic retaliation against those who seek it.

I refuse to have anything to do with such manipulations, and I always remind people of the consequences. But there are those who are so infatuated with a particular individual that they are willing to do anything to obtain their love, a love that is definitely not reciprocated. Turning to dark love is an act that is not tolerated by the laws of the universe or by anyone who is true to their magical workings. The obsessions of those who desire it have blinded their better judgment, as they think they deserve to have someone else against that person's will.

I tell those who seek it that this type of magic will never last—even if the universe decides to grant their desire due to one of many reasons, perhaps simply to provide a learning experience. I want to stress again that dark love never lasts. The bewitchment wears off! When that happens, the manipulator and the individual who conducted the dark-love spell for money must answer to the universe and the Goddess! A lesson should be learned here: don't make a mockery out of love.

I always ask the ones who seek this type of magic, "If this person doesn't love you, why do you want to pursue them?" If I were in that position, I know what I'd do! I'd put on my high heels and look for someone who does love me.

When two people come together, they come together because they were meant to do so. Dark love will never succeed, no matter how much its practitioners try to interfere, because those who try to break the bonds of another's true love will never succeed. If a bond of true love is broken, it will only be broken for a short time; everything always goes back to where it should be—in perfect love and perfect trust for the one for whom the love was meant.

The difference between love magic and *dark*-love magic is very clear, and it's a simple difference to identify. If you are very attracted to a particular person and you feel a connection, but the other person isn't willing to come forward, then that's an example of a time when it's appropriate to practice love magic. Light a pink candle in the name of the person you like. Ask the universe for this person to come forward and tell you their feelings toward you.

If this person comes to you in the next few days and tells you they care for you as much as you care for them, then you'll know it was meant to be; you just hurried along the inevitable. But if the other person tells you they don't want to take it any further, then you must let them go, because that person is not for you.

Now, dark love works differently. If the person you like tells you your feelings are not reciprocated, but you aren't willing to let this person go no matter what the universe says, then you are entering the world of dark love. People practicing dark-love magic may even go so far as to cowardly sneak into the home of another and grab that person's most intimate essences, such as their hairbrushes or even unwashed underwear, in order to take those items to the practitioner of dark love, who will use the essence of the unfortunate love object's soul to manipulate them into submission. The only rationale for this behavior is that the one seeking dark-love magic feels they were denied love—no, not love, but infatuation—from the person on whom they are now preying.

To love someone is to let that person go if they don't want to stay. Nothing is more honorable than to walk away with your head high because you love someone so much that you are willing to let them go so they can find happiness with the person they want to be with. This is love at its best, and it's behavior that should be modeled for those who aren't willing to let go when their hearts are no longer wanted.

Always stay on the right side of karma, working together in unison with the universe. Use love magic in a positive way, to bring only good things to you and your wishes for love.

Anyone can do the fun and easy spells in this book. You can easily tap your love needs and send them to the universe; I can assure you that you will definitely find spells in this book that relate to your present circumstances.

As I've said before, the love spells you choose will be the vessels that carry your love needs to the universe. You have nothing to lose and only love to gain. Who in their right mind doesn't want that?

In the first part of this book, you will learn how to love yourself, the main ingredient in finding and keeping romantic love—there can never be romantic love without self-love. Self-love is the love you have for yourself no matter if you weigh 130 pounds or 330 pounds. It's the love that comes from the pit of your stomach, an unconditional love. Self-love is the acceptance of your decisions and actions, allowing you to attract romantic love. The good news is that a little love magic can help you learn to love yourself!

After you read this book, I predict you will find love and keep it. You will be able to understand love magic and use it to your advantage, always in a positive way. You will be able to do attraction spells, love spells, "honey-do" spells, and more. You will heal love and sexually enhance lovemaking. You will be able to heal a broken heart to accept the breakup of a relationship, and move on to make room for another. You will also learn spells for strengthening relationships, and love spells to keep your relationship interesting where it counts! Moreover, you'll discover how to keep your partner happy—and help you with chores around the house.

Blessed be to all who look for love in the pages of this book. May you find it, keep it, and forever hold it.

Ileana

6
GETTING STARTED: THE "LOVE BOX"

The first step to finding, healing, and keeping love is to gather together some magical tools. Fortunately, you won't need anything that is difficult to find in order to do the spells in this book. On the contrary, your local supermarket and home-and-garden center are among your best magical suppliers—not to mention, of course, magic-oriented websites or any New Age stores that may be in your area. As I've also noted in my other books, items needed for magic do not need to be expensive; they just need to be durable and workable.

Depending on the spells you wish to do, it's good to have some items around the house associated with love. Keep these items in a box, preferably a pink one, and label it fondly as the *Love Box*. In your Love Box, you should keep candle holders, maybe four. You should also add to the box pink candles, any size, but preferably long, tapered ones as they are the best for magical workings.

With any candles you purchase for magical purposes, ensure that the color of the candle will remain consistent once the candle begins to burn. Sometimes a candle may appear pink, or let's say blue, but underneath that color the candle is white. Unfortunately, this inconsistency sends mixed messages to the universe, something you want to avoid when doing a spell since your intent needs to be precise and consistent. So make sure that any candles you buy are truly the color called for in the instructions for each individual spell, both inside and out.

While we're on the subject of candles, you should know that there are also star-sign candle colors. Each individual star sign is associated with a color, and you will be using candles of these colors for some of the spells you'll do. On the next page is a quick guide to star-sign candle colors to get you started.

ARIES	March 21–April 19	White
TAURUS	April 20–May 20	Red
GEMINI	May 21–June 21	Red
CANCER	June 22–July 22	Green
LEO	July 23–August 22	Red
VIRGO	August 23–September 22	Black
LIBRA	September 23–October 22	Black
SCORPIO	October 23–November 21	Brown
SAGITTARIUS	November 22–December 21	Gold
CAPRICORN	December 22 –January 19	Red
AQUARIUS	January 20–February 18	Blue
PISCES	February 19–March 20	White

Now back to your Love Box.

It is a good idea to put ribbons in the box. They can be ribbons of any color you like, but make sure that pink and red are the dominant colors, since these are the colors associated with love and passion. You can also add lavender and rose essential oils to the box, as well as rose petals, apple seeds, fresh rosemary leaves, lavender leaves, even crystals such as rose quartz or any others you like that you think are related to love and attracting love.

You can even put in your Love Box a statue or image of your favorite love goddess, perhaps the Greek goddess Aphrodite or the Roman goddess Venus. Even before you finish putting together your Love Box, you will already be sending signals of love to the universe. While you put your box together, your thoughts will be on finding or healing love, so in actual fact you will have done your first spell, the Love Box spell. And don't limit your box to the items I've suggested! Concentrate, and let your thoughts and feelings dictate what else you add to your Love Box that is relevant to your love needs.

When you think your Love Box is ready, keep it in a special place and don't share its contents with anyone. This box is something private between you and the universe, and no one else. You don't even have to tell anyone about it. In fact, sometimes it's preferable that you don't. People question things they don't understand, which can create a negative energy around you. And when you conduct magic, you need all the positive energy you can get.

You need to know about other energies with which you will be working. One of them is our beloved moon—the "lady of the night," as I call it. The moon is very important in any type of magical workings, as we can tap into the moon's energy to obtain that which we want. A full moon occurs when the moon is bright, round, and at its greatest potential; this is a time for any type of magical workings, especially love spells. After the full moon is the waning moon, when the moon starts to decrease. This is a good time to work against opposing forces, such as an old partner who still can't accept a breakup and is making your new relationship hard to get off the ground.

Then there's the new moon, which is hidden and cannot be seen. The new moon is also a good time for all types of love spells. Between the new moon and the full moon, the moon is waxing and growing. As it grows, its potential is endless, and this is a great time to work on enhancing your love and relationship needs—because as the moon grows full so does the love you want and need.

The days of the week are just as important as the moon. Each day has a relationship to a planet, a relationship you will use to conduct magic on the appropriate days. Let's start with Sunday. Its relation is the sun, and Sundays are a good time to conduct healing spells for love. Monday is related to the moon, and Monday is a great day of the week to protect love. Tuesday is associated with Mars, and on Tuesdays you should conduct strength and courage love spells. Wednesday is associated with Mercury; on Wednesdays it is best to conduct spells for communication, as the planet Mercury is the problem-solver of the planets. Thursdays, related to Jupiter, are for legal matters on love. Venus is associated with Fridays, and it is best to conduct love rituals on a Friday. Saturday is related to Saturn; on this day you will be doing spells against negative love forces.

Before you start doing the spells in this book, find a place that is quiet so you can have total privacy to be in tune with the universe and your needs. When you say a specified rhyme or chant for a spell, make sure that it is true to your heart. Believe the words you speak in order to convey your sincerity to the universe. The universe is there waiting to hear your needs, as is our beloved Goddess. She will grant your wishes if they are yours to have, but don't ever get discouraged with magic. It takes time, and you need to be patient because if it's meant to be, it will be and, if not, the Goddess has an even better plan for your romantic love.

The keys to spellworking are to stay positive and to really mean what you want. Sincerity, honesty, and wanting what is best for yourself without hurting others along the way are the most important parts of magic. If you do harm others, you will have to answer to the Threefold Law: "Harm none; for if you do, it will pay you back in threes."

7

LOVE YOURSELF: SPELLS FOR SELF-LOVE

It's all fair and good that you want romantic love, the ever-lasting love about which you have dreamed since you were seven years old. But before you can achieve this type of love, you need to know if you love the most important part of your world—and that most important part is *you*. Yes, you. Because if you don't love yourself, no one else will.

There is a simple test to discover if your sense of self-love is healthy, but don't feel embarrassed in any way when you do this test, and don't laugh! No, don't laugh, as this is very serious stuff. The test is to take off all your clothes and stand totally naked in front of a full-length mirror. See yourself in your birthday suit . . . and start scrutinizing yourself. Let me tell you that you are your worst critic. I know, I've done this exercise. Now, as seriously as you can possibly be, look deep into your own eyes and ask yourself, "Do I love me?"

This is the most difficult question you are ever going to ask yourself, but you need to know whether or not you love yourself unconditionally with all of the faults you *think* you possess. You need to look at the things that bother you about yourself and deal with them. If you can't change them, accept them and let them be a part of your life. Look at every dimple and every wrinkle, every scar and blemish, and accept them into your space and love the person you have become.

If you liked and loved what you saw in front of the mirror as you scrutinized yourself, you will have no difficulties finding the romantic love you've always wanted. But if you truly didn't like what you saw, or if you don't accept yourself for who you really are, then you have a lot of work to do to repair the self-love you lack.

If you feel negative about yourself and the way you look, those around you will also feel the negativity you unknowingly emit; unfortunately, these negative energies have the ability to break or make a romantic love. These energies are like minute beams of light that, when distorted by a negative thought, feel like small electric shocks to others' etheric fields, acting as a repellent.

The etheric field is a projection of pure energy that is all around us. Being within it is similar to being inside a large bubble of light bouncing with vibrating positive energies—but only when it's healthy, only when you feel good about who you are and when you love the person you see in the mirror every day. If you have doubts about self-love or if you have low self-esteem, the etheric field around you will break, and emit those minute electrical charges that repel others.

We are attracted to one another in both physical and ethereal ways. When you first meet someone, that person is of course attracted by your looks—but only for a split second. Physical attraction concerns what we as individuals find attractive, but that attraction can disappear quickly depending on ethereal attraction, or the attraction of the energies we emit. No matter how physically attractive you find someone, if their ethereal energies are filled with doubt, low self-esteem, anger, remorse, or a lack of self-love, then attraction alone is not going to create romantic, everlasting love—because ethereal attraction will always trump physical attraction.

In essence, the people around you feel the insecurities you have. They feel your troubled mind, if it is troubled, and only because they've felt a trickle of your lack of confidence. You can't afford these electrical leaks when they are visible to others' ethereal fields, but the good news is that these types of leaks can be avoided if you start to think positively about yourself and the way you live your life.

THREE WAYS OF REPAIRING AND ENHANCING SELF-LOVE
1. AFFIRMATIONS

Affirmations help to seal the ethereal field from emitting negative and doubtful energies. By doing affirmations, you are affirming yourself, the way you feel about who you are, and the imperfections you think you possess. An affirmation sends your message to the universe, and the universe listens and responds with positive manifestations.

When you do an affirmation, you must believe in what you are affirming. Make sure your affirmations are sincere and from the heart, and that you believe in what you are saying without fear. You are worthy to affirm your wishes, because you want to love and trust yourself and accept who you are.

An affirmation works in the same way as positive visualization. By speaking aloud an affirmation, you trigger your subconscious mind into thinking and feeling positively about yourself. More often than not, people tend to speak and think more negative words and ideas than they do positive ones. Affirming a positive thought enables us to achieve what we want. An affirmation may work straightaway or it may take some time to process through the subconscious mind; it depends on how long you've been thinking negatively about yourself.

Affirmations should be said first thing in the morning, when your mind is at its freshest and not yet polluted with negative thoughts, and they should also be said at any time you wish during the day. Repeat an affirmation right after you think negatively about yourself. Remember that the more you say your affirmations, the more chances you'll have to start thinking positively about yourself. Think of your mind as a computer; you're installing an "I love myself" program and uninstalling an "I don't like myself" program. Always remember to affirm in the present tense. You want to love yourself *now* and for always, not just in the future, because you want romantic love and you want it now.

Affirmation for self-love and acceptance:

I love me because I am me.
Inner beauty resides within me.
I'm the light of love that radiates warmth and self-acceptance.
And the person I'm most comfortable with is me.

2. THE SELF-LOVE POUCH SPELL

Now that you have your affirmation, you are going to put together a pouch that you can carry with you or hang around your neck. It doesn't matter what material you use for the pouch as long as the color is pink.

In addition to the pink pouch, you will need:

- 1 rose quartz
- 1 small piece of blue paper (write on it "I love _____ [your name]")
- Wooden shavings from a sharpened pencil (no lead)
- 1 cooking clove
- 2–3 drops of rose essential oil
- 1 small twig full of rosemary leaves

Once you have gathered all of the above, place each item separately into the pouch. As you put each item in the pouch, visualize self-love and loving yourself for who you are. This may be a good time for you to say your affirmation over and over again. By doing so, you will be sending to the universe your thoughts of love for yourself, and at the same time you will be energizing your pouch. Once you have finished your pouch, wear it or have it with you at all times and at night place it under your pillow.

3. RID OF THE OLD SELF BATH SPELL

A bath is a good way to utilize the water element to its fullest potential. Water is our emotions, the emotions that run through our veins and through our everyday thoughts. These are the emotions we carry deep within us, emotions we keep hidden from the rest of the world. To obtain self-love, you are going to wash out those old thought patterns because there isn't any room for them when you want romantic love.

You will need:

- 1 black candle
- 1 white candle
- 1 teaspoon of olive oil
- 2 drops of rose oil

- 1 tablespoon of wheat germ oil
- ½ cup of rock salt

Rub the olive oil on the black candle and visualize all that you wish to let go about yourself that you don't like. Then rub the rose oil on the white candle while visualizing the love you want for yourself.

Now light both candles and place them inside the bathroom. Draw a warm bath, and add the rock salt with the wheat germ oil to the bathwater. Once you are in the bath, submerge yourself and think of all you wish to let go about yourself. Wet your hair, relax underwater, and let your fears penetrate the water. (But make sure the salty water doesn't get into your eyes or mouth.)

Once you've finished, don't rinse. Pat yourself dry instead. Look at the water, and in the water see all that you have just let go of and never wish back. Pull the plug and wave goodbye to your old ways and smile because you are now a different person, a person who loves who they are. Don't wash your hair or your body for a full twenty-four hours, as you want to stop that which you have just let go of from ever coming back.

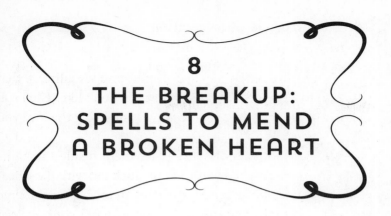

8
THE BREAKUP: SPELLS TO MEND A BROKEN HEART

The breakup of a relationship can be detrimental to your emotional state of mind, and can take you into what I and others call "the abyss." The abyss is a dark, lonely place, uncertain and unfamiliar, filled with your own negative thoughts. After the breakup of a romantic relationship, the emotional pain and exhaustion can leave you totally devastated to the point of no return. Your desire to move on often does not exist. You can't concentrate, your heart no longer beats with life, and the word *love* suddenly takes on a totally different meaning.

Believe it or not, you have created this abyss as a safety zone. Feeling safe within your abyss means that you don't have to face the world and its responsibilities. But the longer you stay in the abyss, the deeper you go into its darkness until you aren't able to focus on anything but your own disappointment.

We've all been there, and I know it's definitely not a pleasant experience. You'll know you've reached the depths of the abyss when physical illness, generated by self-absorption, engulfs your defenses.

The universe knows we all react differently to any specific emotional pain or hurt, but the universe also allows us a grieving period. Embrace this time and use this period to learn and evolve into another stage of spiritual growth. But when you hear a voice telling you it's time to move on, you'll know the mourning hour has now passed and it is time to embrace rebirth.

BABY STEPS

After a romantic breakup, the first thing you need to do is lift your self-esteem because you will not be feeling good about the way you look. Go to the person who styles your hair to ask them about getting a new look, or get a gym membership and start toning your body.

Go through your bedroom and closets, and put anything that belonged to your ex into a box. Leave it in your garage or another out-of-the-way place, and ask your ex to take the box away as soon as possible. Then go through your own things and give away to charity everything you no longer want. You can throw away or burn the items that remind you of memories you'd rather forget, like those old sexy nightgowns you'll need to retire for new ones. Those memories of your relationship are no longer a part of your soon-to-be world.

The next big step is to rid yourself of all of your bedding. Pillows, sheets, blankets—all of it! You've shared your most intimate times in that bed, and it's time to get rid of all that was. If you're financially able to do so, buy a new mattress; if you're not, sprinkle cleaning ammonia, salt, and dry rosemary leaves on the mattress to rid it of all the energies you don't wish to remember. Let that mixture sit on the mattress for about an hour, and then vacuum away the past. Replace the bedding with fresh coverings, preferably in happy and warm colors to keep you cozy. If you do all this, I can assure you that the bed bugs of your old relationship will never bite back.

SPELLS FOR YOUR
EMOTIONAL WELL-BEING
STRENGTH OF STEEL

Moping for a lost love can make you feel weak and lifeless, since you're constantly thinking about the past without making room for the future. This spell will help you find the inner strength you possess, keeping you strong and focused as each day passes.

You will need:

- 1 red candle
- 1 small hollow tube made of steel, with just one hole on the top
- 1 teaspoon of cumin seeds
- 1 teaspoon of poppy seeds
- 1 small piece of parchment paper
- ½ meter (just over 1½ feet) of red electrical tape

Light the red candle on a Tuesday. Then visualize the candle's flame as the strength you'll need to carry you through the day from the time you wake up.

Write your full name on the parchment paper. Then mix together the poppy seeds and the cumin seeds, placing all of them inside the steel tube. As you do so, say:

> *"My physical and mental being*
> *will be as strong as steel from now on."*

With the red electrical tape, close the top end of the steel tube so that nothing inside it can come out. As you tape up the tube, say:

> *"My strength comes from the inside and*
> *the abyss is no longer a part of my life."*

Keep this tube with you at all times—even under your pillow when you're asleep. In a matter of weeks, you'll start to feel stronger; as the days pass, you will feel your strength increase from within.

When you feel you no longer need the steel tube, remove the electrical tape and scatter the seeds to the wind.

LETTING GO

Letting go of the past is the key to imagining the future. What's done is done, and the past is exactly that: the *past*. Once you're able to let go of the past, your feelings and attitudes toward your current situation will change, and you'll be able to confront the sadness you feel. Once you've done that, the pain will lessen, new opportunities will find their way to you, and for the first time since the breakup, your soul can be at peace.

You will need:

- 1 black candle
- 2 blue candles
- 1 frankincense incense stick
- 1 white rose
- A bunch of maple or eucalyptus leaves

Take all of the above ingredients to your backyard or to a park on a moonless Saturday night.

Make a circle with the leaves. When you're done, stand in the middle of the circle. Next, light the frankincense incense stick, placing it in the ground just in front of you. Stare at the night sky and visualize that which you wish to let go that is deeply embedded in your heart.

Now, pick up the black candle and embed your fingernails into it. As you do so, visualize all that you wish to let go. Penetrate the candle with your fingernails, which are acting as your magical pen. Then light the candle, place it outside the circle, and say:

> *"Candle flame now you hold that which*
> *I wish to let go and wish no more."*

Light both of the blue candles and place them inside the circle at each side of the incense stick. While you're doing this, visualize the peace you wish to have and the tranquility that comes from letting go of the things you no longer need.

Now pick up the white rose and gently pass it over your entire body in a caressing manner. See it healing, cleansing, and sealing your soul from ever bringing back that which you've just let go.

Sit outside, still in the middle of your now-sacred circle, for as long as you wish. Outside the circle you've made, watch the black candle burn away the past as you feel newfound peace penetrate your heart chakra (your chest).

Let the black candle burn to its end outside, snuff the blue candles, and pick up all the leaves and scatter them into the wind. Wish yourself a good night, and feel satisfied that the past is behind you and new horizons are ahead.

CALMING THE ANGER WITHIN

Don't blame yourself or the world for what you believe to be your misfortune. First of all, keep in mind that what you're going through is *not* a misfortune. You could blame the entire world for the pain you feel, but doing so will get you nowhere. Instead, think of the experience as another step in your spiritual growth as you move toward a better understanding of love.

You will need:

- A living pine tree
- 2 meters (about 6½ feet) of thick rope
- Pure essential lavender oil

Place four drops of the lavender oil on your hands and quickly rub them together. Next, rub your hands along the length of the rope from top to bottom to distribute the lavender evenly. As you rub in the lavender, visualize the anger you wish to stop and control.

Now, wrap the rope around the pine tree you've found, while saying:

"Pine that keeps the peace within each one of us,
help me to control the anger I now hold.
Don't let me lash out at the ones I love the most
or anyone else."

Tie a knot around the pine tree with the rope. As you do so, visualize the issue or issues that are making you angry. If there is more than one issue making you angry, tie a knot for each one. As you tie each knot, get angry; this is the time you can let it all go! Once you release your anger, you'll leave it in the care of the pine tree and the rope to control.

FORGIVE AND MOVE ON

When you're alone after a breakup, your mind acts like a video on automatic rewind, playing back your relationship and pausing at the scenes you wish you could change.

You must forget the "what-ifs" and concentrate on the "what now." Do this by forgiving the person who matters the most—you! Tell yourself the truth: that you did the best you could do at the time.

You will need:

- As many grape seeds as years the relationship lasted (to get the grape seeds, eat the grapes yourself)
- As many corn kernels as years the relationship lasted
- 1 large cinnamon stick
- 1 rose quartz crystal
- 1 pink drawstring bag

Eat the grapes and leave the seeds together outside in a shady place for one day to dry. When you're ready to start the spell, place the cinnamon stick inside the pink drawstring bag and say:

"Love is who I am."

Now add the corn kernels to the drawstring bag and say:

"I forgive myself for years of self-blame."

Add the grape seeds and say:

"The past shall be erased but not forgotten, and replaced by a future bright and full of love."

Finally, place the rose quartz crystal inside the drawstring bag as you say:

"I replace self-blame with self-love, and this is how it's going to be from now on."

Keep the drawstring bag with you at all times; when you think of the past, touch the bag and your thoughts will be focused on the present. The past will never haunt you.

FORGIVE THE EX

I know you're not going to like this, but you also need to forgive your ex-partner in order to move on. The good news is that you don't have to do so in person. To forgive another when they have done you wrong may seem unthinkable, but you can do it if you step over and push aside your ego. Such forgiveness is a sign of maturity and spiritual understanding. You should also keep in mind that holding grudges often darkens your best judgment and inhibits the healing processes.

You will need:

- 1 white candle
- 1 white flower of any kind
- 1 piece of parchment paper
- 1 blue ink pen

Light the white candle on a Wednesday, and on the parchment paper write the following:

I'm a gentle soul who looks for happiness at every turn.
For actions past I need to forgive what another has done.
No longer will I carry the weight of the past on my shoulders,
because I understand that there are imperfections in all of us.
The quicker I forgive, the quicker I can move on and start
my new life.
I forgive you, [name], *for _____.*

List all the things you need to forgive, and then write:

So be it.

Sign the paper.

Once you've done all that, wrap the white flower inside the parchment paper. Place the paper outside on the grass during a new moon and keep it outside for one entire night.

On the following day, burn the paper and the flower, and take the ashes to the sea. Throw the ashes as far into the water as possible. If you don't live near an ocean, take the ashes to a running stream.

EMOTIONAL HEALTH POUCH

When you are emotionally vulnerable, your health is at risk. The associated pressures from a broken relationship can put your body under enormous amounts of stress. When this occurs, your body will be a magnet for all types of illness—which, unfortunately, you yourself will have emotionally induced.

You will need:

- 1 teaspoon of sassafras
- 1 garlic clove
- 1 teaspoon of dry angelica
- 1 teaspoon of nutmeg
- 1 walnut
- 3 drops of eucalyptus oil
- ¼ meter (just less than a foot) of white cotton material
- ½ meter (just over 1½ feet) of white silk ribbon

Mix the sassafras, garlic clove, angelica, nutmeg, and walnut together, and then add in the three drops of eucalyptus oil. As you mix together all of these ingredients, say:

*"I can't afford to be sick, and sick I will not be
from emotions I carry deep within."*

Follow this by spreading out the white cotton material, placing all that you have mixed together on top of the material as you say:

*"Protected I will be from the invasion of sickness while
dealing with emotions I'm working to control within me."*

Gather together into a bundle the cotton material with the above items inside it. To keep the bundle closed, tie up the top of it with the white ribbon. Keep the bundle under your pillow for protection against any illnesses.

SPIRITUALLY CLEANSING YOUR HOME

Whether or not your breakup was amicable, your home needs a good spiritual cleansing from your ex's energies, which no longer belong there. This cleansing is not hard to do, and it's just another step in the process of moving forward. For the best results, wait and do the cleansing once all of your ex's belongings are out of your home and you're alone.

You will need:

- 1 cup of rock salt
- ¼ cup of dry rosemary leaves
- 1 old white cotton cloth
- 1 cup of ammonia (Do not breath it in!)
- ¼ teaspoon of valerian dry herb on a charcoal tablet (Note: valerian can be hard on the nose)

This spell is best done on a Saturday, when you have some time up your sleeve. Burn the valerian on a charcoal tablet and bring this purifying smoke all over your home—even taking it inside your closets and cupboards. As you do so, say over and over again in a loud and happy voice:

*"New happiness awaits my home
with no negative actions or thoughts."*

Mix together the rosemary leaves and rock salt, and then go all over your residence once more and sprinkle this mixture over every corner of the floor or carpet, saying over and over again in a loud and happy voice:

> *"Strength, faith, and hope*
> *I give my home and all who live in it."*

Moisten the white cotton cloth with the ammonia, and then start from the back of your home and, using the cloth, remove your ex's fingerprints from the windows, doorknobs, or any other place where his or her fingerprints could still be.

As you wipe every place where your ex's fingerprints might have been, say over and over again:

> *"To* [name of ex]:
> *I bid you goodbye and farewell.*
> *Your energies are now gone from my place."*

In a matter of minutes, you will experience a newfound feeling of weightlessness and happiness. Your home will once again be a comfort zone for all.

SADNESS BE GONE

Let's concentrate on your future happiness. Don't think for a minute that you're going to stay sad for the rest of your life! You're going through a grieving period, and the universe, aware of your pain, is allowing you time to reflect, grieve, and move on.

110

You will need

- 2 oranges (cut into six parts)
- 1 lemon (cut into four parts)
- 1 grapefruit (cut into six parts)
- 1 teaspoon of lemongrass
- 4 drops of marjoram essential oil
- 1 yellow candle
- 1 pink candle

Fill the bath with warm water. Then, as you light the candles, visualize the sadness vanishing from your heart. Now add to the bath the oranges, the lemon, and the grapefruit, and watch all of it float to the top. Finally, add the lemongrass and marjoram essential oil.

Mix all these ingredients together in the water, turn off the lights, and get into the bath. While visualizing this bath making your sadness a thing of the past, submerge your head under the water and stay there in total silence for as long as you can hold your breath. Once you surface, all your sadness will be gone and a new happier you will appear in a day or so.

When you've finished with your bath, take the plug out of the bathtub and watch your sadness go down the drain. Collect all the pieces of citrus and place them in the garbage, along with your sadness.

9
SPELLS TO GO

The one simple thing you need to know about love is that it's all around us. Why not try to bring some of that love into your world? You can do so through simple means, which I call "spells to go." These types of mini-spells are simple and easy to do. In this chapter, you'll use natural energies, such as colors, herbs, and even crystals. These energies will bring forth the spirit of love, which will aid you in attracting others into your space.

FOR ATTRACTION
ATTRACTIVE TO OTHERS I WILL BE
Insert a teaspoon of catnip into a small, red drawstring bag and carry it with you at all times. At night, place it under your pillow.

SEXY—NOTHING MORE, NOTHING LESS
Stitch to the back of all your undergarments a small red bow to attract those who see past your clothes.

SWEET LET ME BE
Wear perfumes that are sweet, such as rose, lavender, or vanilla-based perfumes.

CINNAMISH
Carry a stick of cinnamon with you at all times, and chew a little piece when you want to attract the one you like.

FRIDAY AND MONDAY ATTRACTION BATH
Have a bath with a teaspoon of honey and five drops of rose oil every Friday and every Monday.

A PEACH WILL DO

While eating a sweet peach, visualize the love you need. Wash the peach pit in a rose-based cologne and place it outside on the grass on a full moon to draw down the energies from the lady of the night. Afterward, carry the pit with you at all times to attract love into your life.

ELM THE TREE

Wrap your arms around an elm tree and tell it your deepest love wish. When you are ready to leave, pick from the ground any dead leaves; elm trees like their spaces tidy and clean.

CRYSTAL POWER

Carry or wear a rose quartz crystal to attract the love within.

VENUS COMES OUT TO PLAY

Wear pink in the afternoon and preferably red on Friday night, when Venus comes out to play.

LOOK AT ME, LOOK AT ME

Carry a stick of patchouli to attract onlookers.

HIDE AND SEEK

Wash your hair with rosemary and you will be noticed by the one you seek to be with.

RELAX WITH CHAMOMILE

Dip your index finger in a sweet cup of freshly made chamomile tea. As if it were perfume, anoint the pleasure points on your body with the sweet brew to bring yourself luck in attracting those you desire.

BEAUTIFUL

Every morning look at yourself in the mirror and say over and over again as many times as you can in rhyme:

"I am beautiful and attractive to me.
I will be thus to all who look and see."

YO TE ADORO

Carry a periwinkle flower to be attractive and adorable to others.

DREAMS OF LOVE

Burn sandalwood at night and you will have prophetic love dreams of the man or woman you wish to meet.

LET US SHARE

On a full-moon night, share and eat chestnuts with the one you like. Together the night shall pass and love will come around.

ATTRACTION POWDER

In a shady place, dry the skin of a pear you have just eaten. Once the skin is crispy and dry, crush it with a mortar and pestle along with a small teaspoon of damiana until it becomes a powder. Before you go out on the town, dust your hands with this power and you will be attractive to those who make eye contact and hand contact with you.

LOVE WISH

Make a love wish with a handful of sunflower seeds and scatter them in the sea or a running stream.

STAR BRIGHT

Keep a star anise seed with you at all times to bring you the luck you need to find the love of your life.

LITTLE RED FEMALE BAG

To attract women, carry with you patchouli and bay leaves in a little red drawstring bag.

LITTLE RED MALE BAG

To attract a man, carry with you a piece of fresh ginger and a few tonka beans in a little red drawstring bag.

SPELLS TO FIND YOUR ROMANTIC LOVE

The first thing you need to do is to start thinking positively about who you want in your life. Remember that wishes do come true—so when you ask for that special someone in your life, make sure you know what you want. Looks do matter, of course, but personality always outshines looks. Have a clear picture of this person; maybe he or she is someone you already know or someone you've always visualized spending the rest of your life with.

Keep this person in your mind's eye both day and night. By doing so, you are letting the universe know that you are now ready to have what you've always wanted—someone in your life to have and to hold. Visualize this person with you 24/7. Think of what it would be like to be with that person all the time, and keep in mind the things you've always wanted to do with the one you love.

Finding your romantic love is similar to getting ready for an exam. In school, you study and study until you know all the answers by heart; that's also what you'll be doing to find your romantic love. You should think, breathe, and visualize this love until you know the other person as well as you know yourself. As you're doing these visualizations, you're telling the universe that you're ready for romantic love. You want your visualizations to be heard and blessed into a wish for love. No matter which spells you do, visualization is the key in any spell to open the doors to the mystical part of the universe, the mystical part that grants wishes of love.

FINDING YOUR SOUL CONNECTION

Once during every lifetime we meet a very special person, and with that person we feel and make an indescribably strong connection. You can't possibly imagine your life without this other person. This connection is the recognition of souls who have shared numerous lifetimes and have learned and grown spiritually together. With this spell you will find and keep this soul connection.

You will need:

- 1 bag of pink cotton balls
- 1 white candle
- 1 decanter full of fresh water
- 1 bowl of soil

On a Wednesday night when the full moon is out, go out into your backyard or to a park. Make sure there's no wind. Then make a large semicircle around you with the pink cotton balls, and as you do so keep in your mind visions of the person who you know is your soul mate. After you have done all this, stay in the center of the love circle you've just created.

In the middle of the circle and at your feet, dig a hole small enough to keep your candle upright and balanced. Then light it and say:

> *"Light of day, light of night,*
> *search for my soul mate in the flames*
> *of this candle this night."*

Then let the decanter of water spill on the ground four times, and each time say:

> *"Across the seas find the one who is also looking for me."*

Now grab a handful of the dirt, letting it spill on the ground four times. Say each time:

> *"Across land, deserts, and mountains, find my soul mate."*

Once you've finished, sit on the ground with the candle burning just in front of you. Close your eyes and visualize yourself as a bird flying over mountains, water, and land looking for your soul mate, who will soon come to light.

BEFORE A NIGHT ON THE TOWN

If you're single and out having a good time, you can't help but wonder if you're going to meet someone who is worth bringing home to your mother. With this spell, you'll be able to attract and pick the person you'll want to be with for a long time.

You will need:

- 1 red candle
- 1 white rose
- 1 red rose
- 5 drops of lavender oil
- 3 drops of patchouli oil

Draw a warm bath, turn down the lights, and light the red candle. As you light the red candle, think of the fun you'll be having out on the town. Hold both flowers in your hands and let each petal fall gently on your bathwater. Visualize each petal as someone wanting to meet you and wanting to get to know you.

Now, with each drop of oil that you put in your bathwater, say:

> *"To all I meet, come and talk to me*
> *because that is the only way you are*
> *going to get to know and like me."*

Gently step into your now-ready bath and breathe the aromatic essence of love that is penetrating deep into your soul. Relax, because you may be out all night. After your bath, pat yourself dry to seal the energy of attraction you have just created.

ONE DAY A BRIDE I WILL BE

Most every little girl has a dream, and that same dream follows her through adulthood: to get married and live happily ever after. There isn't any reason to believe your childhood dreams can't come true; they *can* come true with this doll spell.

You will need:

- 1 doll, with the same hair and skin coloring as you. This doll must be able to sit down and stand up.
- Enough white material to make the doll a wedding dress
- Tulle to make a veil
- Needle, white cotton thread, and a pair of scissors
- 1 rose quartz crystal

You are going to make a wedding dress for the doll, whom you will call by your own first name. First, design the dress; you can use any material you like as long as it's white. As you design

123

your doll's dress, have in mind the dress *you* will wear on your wedding day.

Tell yourself that the doll is you, and it is you who is getting ready for your wedding day. Make sure not to use a sewing machine, as you must stitch every stitch yourself. It doesn't matter how long it takes you to create your doll bride. You should not be in a rush as you dream of your wedding day and wedding night.

Make the dress first, then the veil. Adorn the doll's hair as you would like your own hair to look at your wedding. Finally, place a rose quartz crystal between the doll's breasts. Sit your doll bride on your bed or stand her up facing the front door of your bedroom. This spell symbolizes you in the future, walking out of your own room all dressed in white on your wedding day.

PICK UP THE PHONE AND CALL ME

By now, you may have already found someone you want to spend time with. But that love interest may not be calling you as often as you'd like to make a date so romantic love can occur.

You will need:

- Pink ribbon
- 1 rose quartz crystal
- 1 tiger's-eye crystal
- 1 glass of water (if you live near an ocean, use sea water)
- 1 teaspoon of rock salt
- 1 small piece of paper

Add the rock salt to the glass of water and submerge both of the crystals in this water. Take the glass out to your backyard and leave it out there for three days and three nights under the stars.

Once you've done this, take the crystals out of the water and rub your hands together until they feel hot and tingly. Then take both crystals into your hands and hold them there, thinking intently of the person you wish would call you. Say out loud:

> *"Remember to call me you will, and other things*
> *I wish you to do to get to know me."*

Write the person's name on the piece of paper, and then wrap the crystals together with the paper and use the ribbon to keep it all in place. Once you've done this, take your little crystal bundle out on a full-moon night and leave it out overnight on the grass. Next, place the bundle by the phone to receive your very important call.

10
RELATIONSHIP
SPELLS

In nearly any relationship, romantic love begins to stagnate at a certain point in time. A busy work schedule can override one's personal life, leaving little time for oneself much less someone else; such a schedule is often a major reason for relationship stagnation. Long-established relationships can suffer not because the partners don't love each other, but because they both begin to take each other for granted. Then there are the unique issues of the young relationship, in which people, such as newlyweds, sometimes try too hard to accommodate each other.

In every relationship, there is always something each partner wants to change or make better; this is normal and, at times, justifiable. We wouldn't be human if we didn't seek change and improvement. If your partner isn't accommodating your needs, your first instinct will probably be to "change" them, but sadly such an effort comes across like nagging. I can assure you that nagging will only jeopardize your relationship. Think about it: the only reason someone in a relationship wants this type of change is to accommodate their own needs, not their partner's.

When you first fall in love, you fall in love with everything the other person brings to the relationship, the entire package. If your partner was a slob before you came along, then there is little you can do to force a change in that behavior if your partner doesn't want to change. Yet when you fully accept your partner for who he or she is, then you'll notice that some changes do happen, and as amazing as it may seem, your partner will start to accommodate your needs.

Communication is a big part of all relationships. Sitting down and talking about what's upsetting you is the key to a healthy everlasting relationship, but there's also no reason why you can't use magic to help yourself through the trying times in relationships and to help resolve the minor arguments all couples have.

RELATIONSHIP SPELLS
I NEED A LITTLE HELP

The last thing you want to do when you get home is house-work, but sometimes your partner forgets that the breakfast dishes are still in the sink. This lack of cooperation can cause tension and can make each of you resent the other.

You will need:

- 1 teaspoon of myrtle
- 1 white candle
- 1 red candle
- Half a teaspoon of lemon rind
- A pair of your partner's stinky socks

On a night between the waxing moon and the full moon, set up a small altar with all of the above items when your partner is away from home. Light the white candle and the red candle together while visualizing what you want your partner to do that will make your life just that little bit easier. As you're visu-alizing, say:

129

"Help me you will without me saying 'please.'"

Mix the myrtle and the lemon rind together. Once you've done this, divide the mixture into two equal parts and gently stuff each of the socks with the resulting halves of the mixture. As you do so, visualize your partner coming home from work and finishing chores without a fuss.

Take the pair of socks and hide them under your partner's side of the bed. Let the candles consume all the way through, and before you know it, your partner will accomplish the little chores and tasks you've always wanted him or her to do.

LIBIDO COME AND WAKE ME!

There's always room for more love in the bedroom. Yet sometimes you're too busy even to think about the pleasures that used to bring you and your partner together. A lack of time is often a factor; by the time you go to bed, you may be so tired that falling asleep is the only thing on your mind. You give your partner a loving kiss on the cheek and say goodnight, leaving your partner, who wanted more than just a peck on the cheek, feeling annoyed.

You will need:

- 2 red candles
- A bunch of holly
- ½ cup of sesame seeds
- 1 teaspoon of honey
- 4 drops of rose oil
- 1 red bowl

Draw a warm bath on a full-moon night just before you go to bed with your partner. Light the red candles in your bathroom and visualize the sexual feelings you wish to have so you're not too tired when it's time to play.

Drop the holly in the bathtub and watch it float on top of the bathwater as you visualize yourself swimming in a sea of passion and lust.

In the red bowl, mix together the sesame, the rose oil, and the honey until a paste is made.

Take your clothes off and rub this mixture all over your body, feeling the aroma and the pleasure it brings you. Now turn the lights down, get into your bath, and relax for a little while.

When you're ready to get out of the bathtub, pat yourself dry. Now, while the candles burn with your desires, slip into bed and be ready for the goddess within you to come out and play. Let the candles do their magic by burning all the way down. Do this spell whenever you feel you need to be a goddess again.

FLAMING PASSIONS

Perhaps you and your partner have been together for so long that passion has become a memory, and it no longer fills up your world. At times you may even think your partner isn't interested in you anymore. Don't worry! This lessening of passion occurs in most long-term relationships; you could even call it a "rite of passage." Such a reduction in passion is destined to occur, but passion can also be reawakened to stir in both of you the feelings you once had for each other, so that you can experience again what once was.

You will need:

- 1 red candle
- ½ teaspoon of vanilla essence
- 2 drops of lilac pure essential oil
- 1 teaspoon of witch's grass
- 1 passion fruit

- 1 teaspoon of honey
- 1 teaspoon of poppy seeds
- 1 small white bowl
- ½ meter (just over 1½ feet) of red ribbon

A week before you do the spell, purchase the large passion fruit and cut it in half. Take out the inner fruit until you are left with only the skin. Place the two halves of the fruit where the skin can dry without sunlight.

On the night you wish to do the spell, place the drops of the lilac oil in the palm your left hand. Then hold the red candle with your right hand. Anoint the candle with the lilac oil by rubbing the candle sensually from the middle of the candle up, then back to the middle of the candle and down, in a slow and deliberate motion. As you do this, remember the passion you and your partner once had. Then, when you're finished and ready to proceed, light the candle.

Combine in the bowl the vanilla essence, honey, poppy seeds, and witch's grass. Mix together well all of these ingredients until a paste is made. (You may need to add in more honey to make this happen.)

Next, stuff both halves of the passion fruit with your mixture. It doesn't matter if any of the mixture is left over. Place both halves of the fruit together to make a whole fruit once again, and to keep it together tie the red ribbon around the passion fruit.

Place the passion fruit in front of the candle and visualize the passion you wish to reclaim. See this passion right before your mind's eye. Keep the candle burning until right to the end. Now, take the passion fruit and place it in your bedroom, under the bed if possible. When you do this, stale passions will become a thing of the past.

You can do this spell on a Friday at any time of day or night.

YOU DON'T LISTEN TO ME

Sometimes you probably feel that your partner is just not listening to you, that the things you say go in one ear and out the other. This lack of communication can cause frustrations, disappointment, and needless arguments.

You will need:

- 1 small bunch of fresh rosemary leaves
- 5 lemon seeds

- 2 cooking cloves
- 4 coffee beans
- 1 yellow candle
- A small piece of paper that you can write on

On a full-moon night, crush together with a mortar and pestle the lemon seeds, cloves, and coffee beans. Once you've done this, write on the small piece of paper your partner's name and the wish you have that he or she will listen to you more closely.

Next, embed the yellow candle with the aromatic mixture you've created; as you do this, visualize your wish to be listened to. Place the piece of paper under the candle, light the candle, and let it burn all through in a place safe from the wind.

MODIFICATION SPELL

If you wish that your partner was just a little bit more accommodating to your needs, you can achieve your desire with this modification spell.

- 1 letter-size (or A4-size) piece of red paper
- 1 blue pen
- 1 red ribbon

The modification you desire can be as detailed as you want it to be, but make sure there's only one thing you wish to modify. Don't confuse the universe with lots of different modifications. This is not a binding spell. A modification simply means modifying a person's behavior without karmic retaliation. Make sure you are honest with your modification, and that you don't try to control the situation or the issue.

The modification could be as easy as "I modify you to be a little tidier around the house" or "I modify you to be more caring toward me," but you can never modify your partner unnecessarily or for domination. Remember that these are white spells, and white spells need to stay white. Modifications are kinder when you don't do a complicated ritual.

On the piece of paper write:

> I, [your name], *modify you*, [your partner's name],
> *to* [modification desired].

Once you've written out your modification, roll the paper into a small tube and wrap it with the red ribbon to keep it in place. Carry this roll with you at all times, and whenever you touch it, the modification will work to your advantage.

HARD TIMES

Tension and disharmony in the home can come about due to rough times or difficult financial situations. This tension can bring terrible stress to any relationship, so that even the littlest things start to make you both miserable and bring nothing but hard times and altercations into your home.

You will need:

- 2 white candles
- 1 sewing pin
- 1 charcoal tablet
- ½ teaspoon of dry rosemary leaves
- ½ teaspoon of lavender
- 2 frankincense small nuggets (similar to those used in churches)
- A photograph of you and your partner during happier times
- Matches or a lighter
- A glass bowl

With the pin, carve your name on one candle and your partner's name on the other. While holding and concentrating on the candle with your name, visualize the hard times you're going through and focus on the inner peace you wish for. Do the same thing with the candle bearing your partner's name, and then light them both.

Now, look at the photo of both of you. As you do so, remember what life was like before your current problems, when the love and bond you both shared was stronger, and wish away the hard times you're currently going through.

Fill up the bowl with sand or dirt from outside. Doing so will protect the glass from breaking once you light the tablet, and it will protect you from getting burned. While you're outside, place the charcoal tablet on top of the dirt or sand in the bowl. Light the tablet until it starts sizzling.

Now, put the rosemary, frankincense, and lavender on top of the charcoal tablet and smell the unmistakable aroma that will bring peace and harmony and will get you both through these difficult times. Bring this bowl all over your home in order to cleanse your home of all negativity.

Once you've finished, place the bowl in front of the photograph and the candles, and let the charcoal tablet sizzle out. Allow the candles to burn all the way to the end for peace and harmony. By the time you've finished this spell, you'll already be feeling the peace within you, your partner, and your home.

YOUR FRIENDS DON'T COME FIRST

If your partner spends more time with friends than with you, you need to do this spell to bring your partner back home and back to you.

You will need:

- 1 candle, the color of your partner's star sign
- 1 sewing pin
- 1 photograph of you
- 1 pair of your partner's shoes

Write your partner's name on the candle with the pin. Light the candle while thinking of your partner coming home to you and not out with friends. As you do so, say:

"Home is where I am and home is where you should be."

Now take the photo of yourself and place it inside your partner's shoes, and home your partner will come to spend more time with you.

Keep the shoes in front of the candle until it burns down, and keep the photo inside the shoes for one full week. Do this spell again every other week for a month, or as often as is necessary.

BUSY AT WORK, NO TIME FOR LOVE

Nobody likes it when their partner works late every night to please the boss. When your partner works too hard, it can put a strain on your relationship, your sex life, and your special family time.

You will need:

- 1 blue candle
- 1 red drawstring bag
- 3 tonka beans
- 3 pecans
- ½ teaspoon of poppy seeds

When your partner is working late, light the blue candle and concentrate on why your partner is working at such an hour. Place the tonka beans, the pecans, and the poppy seeds in the drawstring bag. Tie the drawstring bag tightly so nothing can fall out.

Place the drawstring bag over the candle and let the flames heat the seeds, the beans, and the nuts. As you do this, go clockwise over the flame as many times as you wish and say in a strong voice:

"A hard day's work you have done
and for right now it's enough.
Come home and relax and be with the ones you love."

Place the little red drawstring bag in front of the candle and let it stay there until the candle burns out. Then place the drawstring bag under your partner's pillow where it won't be found. Late nights at work will soon be a thing of the past.

DO YOU LOVE ME?

It's difficult to have feelings for someone but not know where you stand, because the other person isn't in touch with his or her own feelings.

You will need:

- 1 pink candle
- 1 teaspoon of lavender buds
- 1 teaspoon of marjoram
- 2 cherries attached by the same stem
- 1 white shallow plate

Hold the pink candle in your hands and visualize the person you love. Search deep within the other person and bring out the feelings they have for you. Say:

"Search your heart and tell me true the
feelings you hold deep within your soul."

Now light the candle and stand it on the white plate; make sure the candle stays in place by putting a little wax on the plate. Make a circle with the lavender buds and the marjoram around the candle on the plate. As you do this, have in mind the truth you want to hear, be it love or friendship.

Gently hold the two cherries in your hands and place the cherries around the candle without tearing them apart.

This spell can be done whenever you wish, and as many times as you wish, but for maximum strength do it on a full-moon night. Let the candle burn through to the end. Scatter the marjoram and the lavender buds to the wind, and bury the cherries under a flower-flourishing bush.

THE TRUTH AND NOTHING BUT THE TRUTH

The only way a relationship can survive is by being honest and truthful with your partner no matter how bad things are. Remember, you can live with the truth but you can't live a lie.

You will need:

- 1 red candle
- 1 handful of peppercorns
- 1 teaspoon of orange rinds

Light the red candle and visualize the person you think is lying to you. Say:

> *"No more lies will you ever say to me.*
> *Speak the truth and nothing more."*

Rub the peppercorns and the orange rinds in your hands and let them fall gently on top of the candle's flame. As you do this, say:

> *"Lies be gone; be true to your soul and our love."*

Let the candle burn to the end. Put the remaining peppercorns and orange rinds where your partner will never find them.

LET ME GO

If you no longer love your partner for whatever reason, he or she will usually feel betrayed and won't be able to let go as quickly as you have. This sense of betrayal can make the situation difficult for both of you—and can lead to anger, persecution, or even violence from your now ex-partner. Or it could even consume your partner and cause an emotional breakdown.

Don't be angry with your ex, who is going through a letting-go period. Just be patient and remember that you once loved this person. Be as tolerant as you can. By doing this simple spell, you can help your ex through the process of grieving and letting go.

You will need:

- 1 pink candle
- 1 candle in the color of your ex's star sign
- 1 candle in the color of your own star sign
- ½ meter (just over 1½ feet) of pink ribbon

Light the pink candle and send your ex peace of mind and the knowledge that everything is going to be all right. After you've done this, tie together with the pink ribbon both of the candles in your star sign colors and say:

"Once we were tight together like these two candles, but we can no longer be; there is no love for you within me."

Now, with both of your hands, break both candles in half at the same time. The breaking of the candles represents the breakup of your relationship; your ex will finally understand it is futile to continue pursuing you—and will instead get on with his or her life.

11
NEGATIVE
LOVE MAGIC

Once we find romantic love, we don't want anyone to stand in its way or, even worse, to take it away from us. Unfortunately, some people out there use negative magic to steal away the romantic love of others—but you must never let that happen to you!

Those who would use negative love magic against you do so in order to destroy your happiness at all costs. They are obsessive and single-minded in this quest, and they don't care who gets hurt as long as they can get what they want—your romantic partner. When they're obsessed with a particular individual, those who practice negative magic have no scruples or morals and will stop at nothing to obtain their goal.

You can usually tell if your partner has been love-cursed by his or her actions. The first clue comes when your partner starts acting in unusual ways and exhibiting erratic behavior from one day to the next. If you observe this sort of behavior, you'll automatically feel it—but don't confuse negative magical workings with manipulation.

In other words, you need to be certain someone else is really using negative forces against your partner—and that the problem isn't you wanting to keep your partner even after he or she has fallen out of love with you. Make sure you use magic without manipulation. If your partner doesn't love you anymore, then let them go. Remember that to love someone also means letting that person go when he or she no longer wants to stay with you. Why use magic to keep someone who doesn't love you? The only reason someone under such a spell would stay with you is because you've manipulated love.

In order to be certain your partner or loved one is under a spell, and to ensure you're using magic for the right reasons, you must ask yourself the following questions:

- Is there someone in your life at this time who has shown an interest in your partner?
- If there is, has this person been overly friendly and given your partner any gifts?
- Has this person wanted to be alone with your partner and tried to exclude you from any plans the two of them have made together?
- Is this person interested in magic?
- Does this person avoid looking you in the eyes?
- Does your partner talk extensively about this person?
- Has your partner told you that he or she wants a new adventure and is willing to leave your relationship to get it, but isn't sure why?
- Does your partner have an ashen look on his or her face?
- Has your partner lost any personal effects, such as socks, shoes, pants, combs, brushes, or even undergarments? Have these items gone missing without any reasonable explanation?

If you can answer yes to 75 percent or more of these questions, you have a problem that needs to be dealt with as soon as possible. Protecting love is one of the most courageous things you will ever do.

NEGATIVE LOVE MAGIC
STOP IN THE NAME OF LOVE

If someone is using dark-love workings to take away the person you love, this spell is one you have to do.

You will need:

- 1 large piece of paper
- 1 teaspoon of witch hazel
- 1 teaspoon of raw brown sugar
- 1 red ribbon

Write the name of your loved one on the large piece of paper. Place the witch hazel and the brown sugar on top of the name and wrap it all up in the paper. Tie the little package with the red ribbon and place it under the bed of the one you love. Doing all this will make it difficult for anyone else to take away what is yours. This spell will keep your loved one safe in your home and in your bed!

NOT MY PARTNER

Just as you would purchase theft insurance for your home and its contents, so too should you do this spell to keep a person with negative thoughts and intentions from stealing your loved one.

You will need:

- 1 Adam and Eve root
- 1 pink candle
- 1 rose incense stick
- 1 red drawstring bag
- 1 carnelian crystal

Burn the rose incense stick and light the pink candle. While you're doing that, visualize your partner or spouse and think about how deeply in love with each other you are. Now, visualize the person trying to take your partner away from you; in your mind, place an imaginary stamp on this person's forehead and mail her or him all the way to Japan, staying far away from the one you love.

Next, hold the Adam and Eve root and the carnelian crystal in your hand. Run both of these over the smoke from the incense and candle, thinking only about the one you love staying home. Place both the crystal and the root in your little red drawstring bag. Put the bag under your partner's pillow, and the one trying to steal away your love will soon be packing up and going away.

TAKE YOUR EYES AWAY FROM MY LOVER

Sometimes one particular person wants what is yours and will go to any lengths to get it. Don't just stand there and watch this sham take away what you have built and know to be honest and true. Before you do anything, trust your partner. But if you find that the other person is still trying to take away what is yours, you have every right to protect your relationship.

You will need:

- 1 black candle
- 10 peppercorns
- 1 small blue cloth

Light the black candle while you visualize the one who has intentions toward your partner. Embed every one of the ten peppercorns deep within the candle's wax. With each peppercorn you embed, say in a loud voice with strength and courage:

"Keep away from my love, [the name of your partner]! You can't have him [or her] and you never will."

Once you've finished, snuff out the candle and wrap it up in the blue cloth. Doing so will cool the other's passion for the one you love. Place the cloth and candle inside your freezer and keep them there until the issue is resolved in your favor.

PEACE

Negative energies need discord and arguments in order to feed, and they will never be able to penetrate your home as long as there is peace within it.

You will need:

- 1 white candle
- 5 cooking cloves
- 1 teaspoon of rosemary leaves
- 1 charcoal tablet
- 1 bowl filled with sand

On a moonless Saturday night, light the white candle while thinking only about the peace and protection you want in your home. Then go outside and light the charcoal tablet on top of the sand in the bowl. Bring the bowl back inside when the initial smoke has dispersed and a red charcoal tablet has been left on top of the sand.

Now add three of the cloves and sprinkle half of the rosemary on top of the charcoal tablet. By now, you'll be able to see and smell the aromatic smoke, and sense the protection it provides.

Carry this bowl around your residence in a clockwise direction; you are spreading protective and peaceful energies all around your home. When the smoke begins to die down, put the remaining cloves and the leftover rosemary on top of the charcoal tablet.

Repeat this spell every Saturday and Tuesday for as long as you need to protect the peace in your home from those who would take it away.

GET RID OF BAD LUCK FROM THE PAST

Get rid of the wrongs imposed by another, as these are harmful to your relationship.

You will need:

- 1 sewing pin
- 1 teaspoon of olive oil
- 1 black candle
- 1 green candle

You must first recall when the bad luck started in your relationship. When you have an approximate date in mind, place a few drops of olive oil in your hands and rub them on the black candle from the center up and then from the center down.

Take the pin and etch on the black candle the date the bad luck began, followed by a dash and the date on which you are performing the spell. On the green candle, write the current date with the same pin, followed again by a dash. This time, after the dash, write the year 2199.

Light the black candle and visualize it burning to the end and melting all the bad luck in your relationship. Then light the green candle as you visualize your relationship as it once was—full of life, love, and luck.

Let both candles consume all the way to the end. You can do this spell on a full moon and at any time on a Saturday.

12
RELATIONSHIPS AND LOVE HEALING

Love is beautiful, but at the same time it can be emotionally exhausting. Some take for granted love that is so freely given. Others abuse the love they receive without respect or consequences. Then there are those who never say no to love even if they are in an abusive relationship. But there are also people who are quick to let love go without fighting for it because they lack the energy to keep working on the relationship.

Most people in an abusive relationship (even one that is verbally and not physically abusive), or a relationship with an alcoholic, must let love go for their own good and for their own peace of mind if their partner is not willing to seek outside help to save the relationship. Yet if both people even in these types of relationships are willing to work at it and seek counseling, then there still may be a chance to save the relationship. But if your partner isn't willing to take that extra step, then you'll need to accept that you must let go of love for your own good.

A dear friend of mine fell in love with a drug addict. He actually told her he was an addict during the first couple of weeks they were dating. My friend believed that he would give up drugs for her since he loved her. Well, this man did try to quit drugs and took all the necessary steps to start his rehabilitation, but he just wasn't ready. Every time my friend found out that he had lied to her and was taking drugs behind her back, it cost her pain and much anguish.

Here they were, these two people deeply in love with each other, but my friend knew she could not help her boyfriend at that point, and so she finally walked away from him. They kept in touch, but they both realized it was impossible to even try a relationship while he was still abusing drugs.

I always used to tell my friend that if it's not meant to be in this lifetime, it will be in the next. The good news is that this man has since then truly given up drugs, has been drug-free for years now, and he and my friend are now living happily ever after.

Sometimes we have to walk away from these types of relationships for our own mental stability. My friend is one of many people in such a situation who did the right thing; she walked away from her boyfriend to let him deal with his own demons. If a relationship is meant to be, it will be—no matter what steps you take to get there. And if it's not meant to be, then the universe has a better plan for your romantic love. This goes for all types of difficult relationships. It's hard to walk away from them because the love you feel for the other person pulls you to a point at which you can't see the wrongs that are affecting you. For this reason, people say love is blind—and it *is* blind. Everyone around you can see the problem, but you are blind to it because you are in love.

The cluster of spells in this chapter will help you to stay strong and get through the trying times in a difficult relationship; I assure you there will be a spell here that's relevant to your situation. Always seek out a true friend when you are troubled or lost, or go to a counselor for professional help and advice. Remember that no matter how difficult the relationship is, there is always a way out if you want it. *You* are in control of your life.

Search your heart and don't let others pull you down to their level. You are special and deserve the best in life and love. Never forget that.

HEALING
HEAL THE LOVE WITHIN

All relationships are governed by emotions. Once we've been hurt by the one we love, we can spend weeks or even months trying to get over that emotion and the resentment we feel toward our partner. Whether the situation is your fault or theirs, there is healing to be done.

You will need:

- 1 pink candle
- ½ cup of pineapple juice
- 1 teaspoon of blue food dye
- The petals of a white flower
- 1 dash of rose or lavender water
- 1 teaspoon of rock salt

Prepare a warm bath, preferably on a Friday. When you're ready to begin the spell, light the pink candle and visualize the wrongs done to you burning away to nothing.

160

Slowly add the rest of the ingredients to the bathwater. Let the water absorb everything you are putting in it while you visualize peace, happiness, and forgiveness in your heart. Once you've done this, submerge yourself in the healing water and feel its essence traveling to the center of your soul and washing away all your hurts.

Stay in the bath for as long as you like. When you're ready to come out, pat yourself dry, which will seal the healing energy within you. Don't shower or rinse again for a full twenty-four hours.

UNDERSTANDING AND FORGIVING INFIDELITY

Infidelity is one of the hardest things a relationship will ever have to face, but romantic love can sometimes survive it—even though the pain of the betrayal may not diminish and your sense of trust may not return to what it was before.

The first thing you need to ask yourself after discovering infidelity is whether or not you want to work to forgive this betrayal. If you do, then ask your partner if he or she is also willing to put the infidelity behind you both and work with you on mending the wrongs done. If your partner is willing to take this path, then you must resolve to work to forgive, understand, and move on without bringing up the infidelity at every turn.

You will need:

- 1 teaspoon of nutmeg
- 1 teaspoon of angelica
- 1 teaspoon of palm oil
- A mortar and pestle
- 1 blue candle
- 1 candle in the color of the star sign of the person who was unfaithful to you (see page 81)
- 1 sewing pin
- 1 photo of you both together in happier times
- Pink and blue ribbon (from your Love Box, if you're keeping one)

On a Sunday morning when the sun is out, mix together the nutmeg, angelica, and palm oil with the mortar and pestle. Add more palm oil if you need it to make a thick paste. On the blue candle, etch your name with the pin. Next, anoint the candle with some of the healing, loving paste you've just mixed together. As you do so, visualize yourself forgiving the pain and suffering caused by the infidelity. Also visualize your heart's willingness to forgive and move on.

Now pick up your partner's star-sign candle. Use the pin to write your partner's name on that candle as you visualize him or her fully devoted to working on your relationship and never hurting you in this way ever again. Anoint this candle with the healing paste you've mixed, but this time only add the paste to the bottom half of the candle, the half farthest away from the wick end. As you do this, visualize your partner never straying again.

Hold the photo of you both in your hands and then place it over your heart, visualizing happy times once again. Anoint the photo with the rest of the paste. Once you've done all this, roll up the picture. To keep the photo rolled up, wrap the pink and blue ribbons around it with six knots. Place the rolled-up photo in front of the candles.

Light the candles and visualize the hurt and suffering subsiding, allowing you to understand and move on. Let both candles burn through right to the end. Once they've burned through, take the photo and put it under your mattress on your partner's side of the bed. Don't remove it from there until you're comfortable that the necessary healing has occurred.

SEEK AID FROM AN
ADDICTIVE RELATIONSHIP

There are different types of addictive or dysfunctional relationships, but they all have one thing in common: they hurt whoever is in them. You must be the one to break away from the never-ending cycle of dysfunction, whether it is a cycle of verbal or physical abuse, out-of-control jealousy, or something else such as alcoholism or drug addiction.

If you are in this type of relationship, you need to ask yourself: Do I need this? Am I strong enough to handle this relationship? Do I want to stay in this relationship even though I know there isn't much light at the end of the tunnel? You must be honest with yourself and remember that every dysfunction and addiction comes from a refusal to face a possibly painful past.

Face the facts: if your partner refuses to seek help, then he or she is preferring to drown in self-pity. If you think you can help such a person even after a refusal of professional counseling, you are wrong. Your partner must acknowledge that there's a problem that's damaging the relationship before you'll be able to help him or her. Even if there may be hope for both of you down the road, you don't need to watch your partner destroy his or her life or your own. Sometimes you really must leave the one you love for the good of both of you. This spell will help you to get in touch with the inner you as you seek support and direction from your guides.

You will need:

- 1 white candle
- 1 glass of fresh water
- 1 white flower

At a time when you're home alone and no one could possibly disturb you, gently drop the petals of the white flower into the glass of clear, fresh water. Place the white candle next to the glass of water. Now, light the candle and watch the candle's flame burn.

Think of your guardian or your angel, whichever one you believe is always by your side, and seek his or her help. Say out loud:

"I seek the wisdom of those who care for me
to help me find the answers to my addictive love.
If I should stay or go is the wisdom I seek within you and me.
Help me find the answers and let me be true to my heart and

the ones I love with all my might.
I seek peace to move on, or strength if I should not.
Let me uncover the answer I seek,
so as not to be addicted to an unhealthy relationship."

Once you're finished speaking, reflect on what you've said and listen deep within your soul. Your answers will come as the days pass by.

Let the white candle burn right to the end and place the glass of water with the white flower petals in a high place, so that no one can touch it before the answers you are seeking arrive.

CLOSING

When you find love, keep it. But if you lose it, it will find you again. Hold on to your soul mate. If you don't find your soul mate in this lifetime, you certainly will in the next. Never lose hope, as love is nearby. Be true to your heart, and don't stay where your love is no longer needed. Remember, there is another love waiting around the corner who will hold you and keep you breathless forevermore in this lifetime and the next.

Blessed be,
Ileana

WHITE SPELLS

FOR PROTECTION

INTRODUCTION:
STRIKE ME NOT

Strike me once, strike me twice,
but never shall you strike me
a third time around.

If a total stranger, or even someone you knew, came to your front door and for no reason suddenly slapped you in the face, how would you react? At first, you'd probably be confused about what had just happened. But before you had enough time to react, imagine that you got slapped once again. Now you're no longer shocked and a hidden anger stirs deep within you. You ask yourself, "What have I done to deserve this?" when suddenly you see the hand ready to strike you once again. This time you are aware and ready to protect and defend yourself. This time you reach out and hold the hand before it has time to strike you, saying "Don't you ever hit me again!"

Protection and defense magic works similarly. It kicks in when enough is enough and it's time to start diminishing those negative energies by catching the bullet before it gets you. Protection and defense magic is not about revenge. It's about looking after yourself when others are trying to harm you with magic.

When performing defense magic, you must always take karma into account. The laws of karma should be respected at all times. The universe is well aware of those inflicting physical or emotional harm against innocent souls by means of negative magic. When such an injustice is committed, it is known to the universe—and the perpetrator is paid back threefold.

Unfortunately, we don't know when the universe will justify others' wrongs. The process could take weeks, months, years, or it could even go toward that individual's next lifetime. In the meantime, you sit and wait. While you do, the negative soul gets away with all types of injustices toward you or your loved ones.

You have every right as a member of the universe to protect yourself against these types of people; you don't have to just sit there and take the injustice. Act wisely and use protective and defensive magic.

If you have a problem using this type of magic, think of it as an alarm system for your home to keep intruders from entering and taking what is yours. Remember that such people deserve no pity. They certainly have none for you when they start to use destructive forces.

Never feel guilty when using white spells. We are all human, and it is human instinct to protect our territory from danger and against negative individuals who only want to inflict emotional or physical pain. If your heart is pure, you could never do anything against the laws of karma or against a fellow soul member.

Positive thoughts create loving, healing energies while negative thought patterns can be classified as curses—curses that are potentially very harmful to any individual at whom they're aimed. The funny thing about negative thought patterns is that the people who produce them are sometimes unaware of doing so, which means such negative thoughts are often transmitted very innocently to someone who doesn't deserve them. Yet others are well aware of their negative thought patterns and transmit them very viciously in order to cause harm intentionally.

Such individuals carry with them a negative obsession to destroy whoever they "believe" has done them wrong. Their thought patterns are filled with malice but can only produce destructive energies when directed toward someone else. These people will stop at nothing to destroy you.

Their greed is driven very passionately by their egos in order to manipulate others whom they consider to be weaker. They do this to obtain control and to cause harm and destruction to anyone who gets in the way of their own goals.

Thoughts directed toward anyone in such a negative manner do penetrate the aura field, more so when physical defenses are down due to stress or illness. Such factors can make you even more vulnerable and susceptible to negative thoughts. You become like a sponge, unconsciously absorbing negative thought forms that are hanging over you just waiting to strike you down.

The sad part is that the person sending you all these negative thoughts has no moral conscience and doesn't care about your well-being. Such a person might be disguised as your neighbor, one of your relatives or co-workers, or even your best friend. Always be aware. Your gut feeling never lets you down and you will know who the carrier of negativity is.

Eventually, you'll begin to ask yourself what you've done to this person to make him or her act this way. Well, you may have done absolutely nothing. He or she may not even know what you have done but may nonetheless be filled with an unknown hatred toward you while battling with internal insecurities and jealousy. Such people are carrying a negative obsession against you, which has lodged itself in their corrupted minds, and they will stop at nothing until their negative thoughts result in physical or emotional harm.

During my years of experience helping others to protect and defend themselves against these types of injustices, I have come to the conclusion that people who seek this type of destruction toward another soul are often out to destroy happiness at any cost.

Unfortunately, if they aren't able to accomplish what they set out to do with negative thoughts and actions, frustration sets in and it is at this point that some seek magic to finish the job. You may be asking, "What type of magic?" Well, in the world of magic, there are corruptive forces that I call "the malignant tumors of the occult."

The malignant tumors are not your everyday true practitioners; they are out there practicing destructive magic—that is, if the price is right. These people should not be categorized with those who have personal pride in their magical workings. Everyone who practices true magic is well aware of those who certainly do not.

We have all experienced sadness in life and all of us appreciate laughter when it comes around. Magic is the same way: black or white, positive or negative, you need to have experienced both to know the difference. For example, let's say that you could wish death on a person by lighting twenty black candles, aiming destructive thoughts toward the person. With positive protective and defensive magic, the magic could work in reverse. You could light pink and white candles to wish a person peace within while also asking him or her to leave you alone. There is a difference; it's how you practice magic that makes you a true practitioner, and without that understanding there can never be a balance to the soul.

Sadly, many people have the wrong idea about magic. The Hollywood image has been a damaging one and it is only beginning to change. We witches don't have big noses covered in warts but are beautiful people with intelligence who possess goodness in our hearts. This reality is slowly coming across.

Just because magic is practiced does not mean that it is negative, destructive, ugly, or evil.

I am deeply concerned when people approach me to conduct their dirty workings. An example: a few years ago, a lady who had been having an affair with a married man for about six months came to see me. The man had left this woman because he still loved his wife and wanted to make their marriage work. This woman was beside herself and wanted me to break up their marriage so he would go back to her. I tried to reason with this woman for more than an hour but she wouldn't listen to anything I had to say and told me flat out, "If I can't have him, neither can she!" and walked out. I heard through the grapevine a few weeks later that she paid five thousand dollars for someone to do her negative workings. I felt sorry for her, and the person who took her up on it, and sent protective loving energies to the married couple.

Like this woman, hundreds of thousands of people are out there looking for someone to do their negative workings. Once they find this person, they don't ask moral or ethical questions. They only discuss destruction to an innocent soul and the cost involved to start the dark workings, money that is often paid willingly even when the price is a small fortune.

The most common form of black magic practiced is the application and manipulation of essence, when a part of someone—a piece of clothing, a strand of hair, nail clippings, a photograph, or another sort of personal item—is stolen and used. Such an item is taken to the person conducting the negative workings, who now has a piece of the subject's essence and generally uses it to weaken the aura field. This is one of the worst types of manipulative magic as it works against one's own energies, the essence of one's soul.

When the manipulation of essence penetrates the aura field, it may manifest in lack of energy or sleep, a loss of finances, a sudden unexpected illness, disharmony in the home, bad luck, accidents, a feeling of being lost and unloved, hair falling out, or the end of a strong, years-long relationship.

Mental and physical strength is the first ground rule for working against negative forces. If you feel sick, act as if you're on top of the world. If you know that someone is working against your own energies, then it's not the time to seek sympathy from others. This is very important. If the negative source finds out you have been ill, then your defenses are down—and that is when they strike the hardest. The negative source may find out about your illness when someone you know, or the friend of a friend, feeds them the information. It could all be very innocent but, before you know it, the information gets back to the person working against you.

Some of the things that are done are horrific and hard to believe. I have witnessed some of the most sickening and selfish aspects of human nature, and there is no turning back once someone is on that path of destruction.

These people tap into spells that would make your hair stand on end: spells to bring illness to a victim, to separate a man and a woman or to break up a marriage, to attract another against his or her will, or to break a mother's heart by turning her children against her. Or they might invoke curses to give someone an ulcerous tumor, to intentionally harm someone with the use of wax dolls, to destroy a business, to cause fights in the home, to force the loss of a home from lack of finances, to seek vengeance from someone, or to steal others' psychic gifts. Others try out sexual curses to leave a man impotent, to bring bad luck, or to manipulate a lover. Some have even cast a spell to blind or silence a dog.

Now you can understand why protection is needed against these types of spells, which are dangerous to anyone they're aimed at. Imagine if you had no way to fight back against this type of injustice; it would be like a home invasion during which you are helpless to retaliate and your life is at the whim of others who can, at the very least, leave you emotionally scarred forever.

13
MAN AND UNIVERSAL LAW

DEFENSE AND PROTECTION

It is very important to know how to defend and protect yourself against negative forces. The key to overriding this type of magic is to be aware, to know how to defend yourself, and to know when to do so.

Our own individual upbringings and beliefs as well as the larger society have engraved on our subconscious that taking justice into our own hands is "wrong"—and rightly so. We have no right to take the law into our own hands and to judge others for the wrongs they have done. This is the "human law," the law that keeps the masses under control for the good of society.

But we are also participants in a universal law, to which we all hold a free membership. As acting members of the universe, we all have the right to protect and defend ourselves and our loved ones against any type of injustice, whether it comes from a negative source or the mugger down the street who hits us over the head and takes our money. Just as you would seek justice by taking the mugger to court, so you can do the same with those sending negative thoughts your way.

The human law and the universal law are very similar in many ways. The human law is there to protect us and to defend the innocent; this is also the purpose of the universal law, but with it you have to protect yourself, too. If your home were broken into and you didn't have an alarm system or property insurance, then you'd be at a loss. The law can try to catch the thieves and you would ideally retrieve some of your personal items, but we know very well that doesn't always happen.

After such a robbery, you tell yourself it won't happen to you ever again, so you install an alarm system and buy property insurance. The law can help you, but you also have to help yourself and protect yourself against such an injustice.

The universal law works the same way. As I've already stated, the universe is aware of anyone who inflicts unnecessary physical or emotional harm by means of negative magic. But you still need to protect and defend yourself against any type of negative magical workings.

You have every right to protect and defend yourself against any type of injustice. Think of such protection as an alarm system for your home that will stop intruders from taking what is yours and hurting you and the ones you love.

At some point in our lives, most of us have needed to protect and defend ourselves from a bully of some sort or have defended ourselves against an unfair accusation. Even Disney movies show us how good always confronts and defeats evil, always with magical endings filled with happiness, hope, and everlasting love.

You can fight back if dark occult forces are out to get you. There is always a will and a way, and your will and way will be much stronger than theirs. Yours comes from the heart; theirs is completely filled with hate. I can assure you that karma is on their tails every step of the way—whereas the universe is your knight in shining armor, there to protect you.

14
HAVE YOU
BEEN CURSED?

Don't always blame magic for your misfortune. There are numerous types of curses that we inflict upon ourselves, and these are very similar to those that come from others.

This is why it is so important to analyze even the smallest hiccup in your life before blaming it on someone else. Remember that we do have the right to defend ourselves, but not to accuse someone unjustly. This is where the hard work starts. You need to ask yourself the following questions:

1. Are you feeling tired or ill for no reason?
2. Do you feel life is not worth living?

3. Is your hair falling out?

4. Is there a personal item missing?

5. Has your financial situation changed in the last three months?

6. Are there more than the usual misunderstandings in your home?

7. Have you lost your job?

8. Are you unable to find work?

9. Have you become accident-prone and had a stream of bad luck?

10. Is your marriage or relationship falling apart for no reason?

11. Are you unable to find love in your life?

12. Is everything you do going wrong for no valid reason?

If you have answered "yes" to about 75 percent of the questions, you could be under some type of negative influence, but we can't just stop there—let's do a bit more detective work. Make a list of friends and family that visit your home or workplace often. Divide the list in two columns, a positive one and a negative one.

After you finish the list, have a look at your negative column and I'll bet you there is a person on that list who visits and leaves you completely without energy. We all have one of those friends. These sorts of friends are called "vampires of light." They will even tell you, "I feel so good when I talk with you." They're harmless; they just need light that they can't produce for themselves because of their own lack of self-esteem, which is why they feed from your own supply, leaving you mentally exhausted.

The next person on the list could be someone from your place of employment—a boss or a co-worker. These people may feel some type of jealousy toward you and wish they had your work abilities, or they might be jealous that you got the promotion they'd wished for. They could willingly be sending negative thought patterns to you, which can become an issue for protection in your place of employment.

Then there is the family friend or family member who you really don't want to have around. This person could be harmless, but there might be a clash of personalities. Or he or she could be someone you've just never particularly gotten along with or liked. You need to judge if this person has gotten over your disagreements, and if they haven't, they need to stop sending all those negative thoughts to you. This issue should be addressed and stopped with protection.

We also have many acquaintances. We talk and have fun with lots of people, but true friends are hard to find. Yet we all generally know at least one person with whom we share our thoughts and feelings, and this person should be treasured. If you've counted more than five close friends, then check your list again and find the friend who always says, "I'm there for you"—but actually isn't. This one could be the thorn you have been looking for but never knew existed.

By the same token, this person could be someone who starts rumors and quietly tells your partner something you did, changing the story so that it is very different from what you remember. This person could also be in love with your partner, with thoughts that are no longer friendly toward you; unfortunately, those thoughts could be starting to penetrate your aura field. If there is anything missing from your home and this person was the last one to visit, then there is a good chance he or she is up to no good. In this case, protection is a must before this person breaks up your home and your relationship by manipulation of essence.

The next person on the list could be someone who taps into occult forces. Just be aware, and make sure they only practice positive magic. You can tell if they do; something about their aura is always clean and welcoming. If you don't feel this, this person could very well be practicing negative magic, especially if they talk of vengeance and payback. If that is the case, stay away. These people are not mature enough to understand that there is spirituality in all magical workings.

Then there are self-inflicted curses that do not necessarily result from negative occult forces. These curses can be broken, and they must be dealt with in order to move forward and find a better understanding. If you're dealing with such a curse, you need to stay positive and work on personal issues or your issues around the other people who are holding you back from your own spiritual growth.

To break any type of curse, you can start by ignoring all negative written material that you come across, including chain letters. These are "seal curses," and they penetrate the subconscious mind. Just ignore them and don't give in to them. If you do give in to them, you will make the curse manifest. It's best to burn the letter and sprinkle salt on top of the ashes. As for chain letters, just throw them away. Remember that if you give in to such a curse, you will make whatever was written happen.

Stay away from people who use "perpetual curses." These curses are inflicted by partners, parents, or others who are close to you and are physically or verbally abusive. People who are constantly telling you that you are worthless and will amount to nothing without them will naturally make you feel timid and scared, and make your natural defense system collapse. They have actually cursed you. This curse is easy to overcome once you take the first step by physically walking away from those who have cursed you and seeking professional aid.

There are other curses like the "unforgiven curses" that are carried from past lives. You can break these by doing meditations and past-life regressions to find out how you can fix the wrongs of your past life in this lifetime. Other things that you may feel are holding you back such as, for example, fear or a phobia, also hold back your spiritual and personal growth.

Don't blame others for the "curses within." By not feeling good about yourself, you—and you alone—are responsible for these curses. Believing that you are too fat, too skinny, or "just plain ugly" is a type of curse and you will need to do some positive visualization about yourself to find the truth behind this self-hate within you. This curse can be reversed by programming your subconscious mind into always thinking in a positive way about who you are—a child of the universe with inner beauty that comes straight from the soul.

We should treat our minds like computers. Everything we want, we should keep and what we don't want, we should trash. But the hard drives in many people's minds are always full. Such people hold on to emotions like hurt and sorrow, and in so doing fill up their hard drives, which then don't allow them to experience new and wonderful things because they are full of trash. Empty your hard drive and transfer that which you wish to forget to a disk so you can always open it if you wish. File the rest in your hard drive and save it as "joy and happiness.doc."

Just remember, if you think you have been cursed, you will be, so stay positive at all times. The more you think about the curse, the more those who have cursed you will be able to intrude on your spiritual space. Don't let them; you are stronger than they are. You have the goodness of the universe on your side, and it will not let any injustice into your sacred space if you are willing to fight back.

15
GETTING
STARTED

You need a place to conduct your magical workings. A bedroom or the living room in your home is fine. The place itself isn't important; just make sure that you can work without being bothered by family members or roommates. It's always better to do your magical workings alone and in private, unless you specifically want or need someone else to be there. The reason is very simple: some people don't understand, and they judge without knowledge. Their judgment can be very detrimental to any magical working, and could scatter the energies you wish to send out to the universe. Another's negativity about what you are doing and trying to achieve will affect the direction of your energies, and your thoughts will not reach the desired destination.

Once you have found a place to conduct your magical workings—let's call it your sacred site or altar—you should set up a small table. (A card table is good, as you can fold it up when it's not in use.) There is no right or wrong way to set up your sacred site; just do it according to your tastes, faith, and beliefs.

There are numerous items needed, and energies used, to conduct spells. It's always good to have all the items that you might need at hand, or at least to know what these items are—and to be able to understand why they are used.

ALTAR SUPPLIES
CANDLE HOLDERS

Sometimes, you will be using a few candles at the same time, so it's always good to have many candles around. You can purchase inexpensive candle holders, there's no need to go to great expense. Brass candle holders can tarnish and look disagreeable; and if your candle holders look bad, you might not remain focused on your magical workings.

CANDLES

The colors of candles are very important in any type of magical workings. Each color has a magical meaning and is used to promote and enhance that particular desire. When you purchase a candle, make sure that the candle colors described on the outside of the box are the same as the actual colors of the candles inside. Also, if a spell requires a blue candle, you should ensure that the candle burns all blue—and not white in the middle and blue on the outside.

Candles need to be dressed if you are using them for a magical purpose. For any type of magical intent, the candle is divided into two parts. From the middle of the candle up toward the wick is called the *North Pole*, and from the middle down to the end is the *South Pole*.

When a spell indicates that you should dress the candles, you must rub each candle with the oil specified in the spell. Rub a bit of the oil in both of your hands. Encircle the candle with your right hand and bring that hand from the center of the candle up the North Pole of the candle. Next, encircle the candle with your left hand and bring that hand down from the center of the candle along the South Pole of the candle. Never rub both of your hands simultaneously in an up-and-down motion.

You can dress the candles with olive oil, unless the beginning of the spell specifies differently. Always visualize the task at hand when you are getting the candles ready for magic.

There are also astral-colored candles you will use when a spell requires a candle in a specific person's astral color, according to his or her star sign.

ASTRAL COLORS		
Aries	March 21–April 19	White
Taurus	April 20–May 20	Red
Gemini	May 21–June 21	Red
Cancer	June 22–July 22	Green
Leo	July 23–Aug. 22	Red
Virgo	Aug. 23–Sept. 22	Black
Libra	Sept. 23–Oct. 22	Black
Scorpio	Oct. 23–Nov. 21	Brown
Sagittarius	Nov. 22–Dec. 21	Gold
Capricorn	Dec. 22–Jan.19	Red
Aquarius	Jan. 20–Feb. 18	Blue
Pisces	Feb. 19–March 20	White

CANDLE SNUFFER

Candle snuffers are a must. Candles should never be blown out because, in doing so, a spell immediately loses its intent. And let me tell you: it's no fun extinguishing ten candles with your fingers. Invest in a candle snuffer. Believe me, the money will be well spent.

VASE FOR FLOWERS

A vase is optional. I like to have fresh flowers on my altar at all times, as they keep the room fresh and full of love. It's good to have fresh flowers on your altar, even if just for your daily meditations or positive visualizations.

MORTAR, PESTLE, AND HERBS

You should have a mortar and pestle to use in your kitchen to blend herbs together. In magic, the mortar and pestle are also used to mix and crush different herbs together to cause a desired effect. Herbs are very important in magic. For example, rosemary leaves are not only for garnishing your lamb roast; in magic, rosemary can also be used for protection, intellect, and love. The best mortars are those made of wood.

CENSER AND CHARCOAL TABLETS

You can use a small bowl for your censer, or a tiny cauldron with three legs; it doesn't matter if it's made of metal or glass. You can burn dry herbs on their own by lighting a match to them. Or to get more out of your dry herbs or resins, just fill the bottom of the censer with either dirt or sand—even rock salt—to insulate the container, then place a charcoal tablet on top. It's better to light it outside the house as it initially gives off a not-so-pleasing gray smoke. Then, when it becomes red hot, you can add your herbs on top of the charcoal. Be aware that the charcoal tablets are a fire hazard and should be treated with care. Do not drop them on the floor or use them around small children—the burns are very painful.

OIL BURNER AND ESSENTIAL OILS

An oil burner is not just used in aromatherapy for medicinal purposes or to alleviate stress. Essential oils are often used in magical workings as well, and their strength is concentrated to focus on an intent or to dress candles for magic. Oil burners are usually ceramic, and you should choose one based on your own individual tastes. You may even already have one in your cupboard.

THE PENTAGRAM

The pentagram is a five-pointed star used at times for protection, and while working with and representing the elements.

ELEMENTS

In some of the spells, you will utilize elemental forces for strength and wisdom to aid with the spell. The elemental forces are earth, water, air, and fire. The elements are embedded deep within the soul of every single one of us. They keep us in touch with the self and function in unison with each other to calm the storms in our hearts, and to help us to grow spiritually, to make the right choices, and to have the firepower to fight for what we believe is right.

EARTH (GREEN)

Earth is the grounding force of our needs. It allows us to accept what we have until we reach our desired goal.

WATER (BLUE)

The emotions are controlled by this element. It puts us in touch with past hurts in order to transform that pain into knowledge. It can wash away the deepest hate, and turn it into love and understanding. But most of all, the water element shows us how to forgive.

AIR (YELLOW)

Air lights the light that is deep in all of us. It strengthens our ideas to make them realities. It is the air that we breathe. Without air, we cease to exist.

FIRE (RED)

The fire element is the driving force behind making everything that we need or want come to be. The fire element gives us strength and reason to fight for what we believe and that which we wish to achieve.

COLOR

Color is an essential part of any type of magical workings and should be used whenever possible to enhance that need.

Follow the chart on the next two pages and use color to promote peace, health, happiness, wealth, and protection. You can also wear a color to enhance any actual spell. In doing so, you will be showing the universe what you need.

COLOR	MEANING
Amber	Develops psychic abilities and communication with spirits and guides. Provides a deeper meditation state.
Black	Wards away negativity, removes hexes, protects against evil workings, and promotes truth in magic.
Blue	Brings peace and tranquility, banishes anger, gives protection against others' negativity and unwelcome thought patterns.
Gold	Strengthens the mind. Can be used in money spells and in communicating with the higher realm.
Green	Luck, used for money and self development spells. Heals emotional pain. Helps spiritual growth.
Purple	For third-eye workings and meditation.
Lavender	Peace, spiritual development, and restful sleep.

COLOR	MEANING
Orange	Encouragement, fertility spells.
Pink	Attracts friendship, brings love within to be able to love others and be loved in return.
Red	Strength, power, protection, and courage needed to fight against negative forces.
White	Peace and purity, protection for children and your home. Brings justice, and helps you to work and communicate with your spiritual guide.
Yellow	Understanding, communicating with others, and learning. Sparks the intuition and warns against dangerous situations.

CHAKRAS

The chakras are the healing life force in our bodies and the source of our survival. Chakras can be used in magic to protect or enhance a particular life point. There are seven main chakras; beginning at the base of the spine and finishing at the top of the head, they are:

ROOT (RED)

Located at the base of the spine.

ABDOMINAL (ORANGE)

Located in the lower abdomen.

SOLAR PLEXUS (YELLOW)

Located under the breastbone.

HEART (GREEN)

Located at the center of the chest.

THROAT (BLUE)

Located at the center of the throat.

THIRD EYE (PURPLE)

Located in the center of the brow.

CROWN CHAKRA (PINK)

Located above the head.

CRYSTALS

Crystals also play a big part in magic and are an excellent tool to use with your spells. There are hundreds of crystals out there. If you are unable to identify one, just visit your nearest lapidary association; they will be more than happy to find or identify what you need or have. When crystals are worn, they amplify the etheric body and in turn strengthen your aura field by acting as a coat of steel to protect your sacred space. Crystals need to be cleansed before being used, even if a particular spell does not specify cleansing. The best way to cleanse a crystal is to place it in a mixture of water and a teaspoon of salt. Leave the bowl containing the crystal, salt, and water in your backyard or on your front porch for three days and three nights, after which your crystal will be ready to use and program.

CALENDAR WITH LUNAR PHASES

Most calendars note lunar phases; make sure your calendar does so as well. The phases of the moon are frequently used in magical workings. When the moon is full or new, you can do any type of magical working. You should perform positive spells when the moon begins to wax (increase), and when the moon starts to wane (decrease), you will want to perform spells to get rid of negativity, bad influences, negative workings, and even your own negative energies.

MEANINGS OF DAYS OF THE WEEK, PLANETS, AND COLORS

Each day of the week has a meaning; if you do a spell on a specific day of the week, using the assistance of the planets to guide you and help direct your intent, you will be totally focused and will work in conjunction with the forces of the universe.

DAY	PLANET	COLOR	MEANING
Sunday	Sun	Yellow	Protection, healing the self and illness, money spells
Monday	Moon	White	Psychic abilities
Tuesday	Mars	Red	Courage, leadership, strength
Wednesday	Mercury	Purple	Communication

DAY	PLANET	COLOR	MEANING
Thursday	Jupiter	Blue	Money, legal problems, and personal goals
Friday	Venus	Pink	Love, relationships
Saturday	Saturn	Black	To get rid of opposing negative forces

Now you are ready to start! It is very important to include your positive attitude and visualization to any of the spells you do, as well as to add all the tools already mentioned. Visualizing your needs to the universe is a required part of any magical work. The more you visualize, the stronger the possibility is that the intended desire will reach its destination. Don't confuse protection or defense with manipulation of others; if you do, you will need to answer to karma. Always remember that what goes around comes back around.

16
TOOLS FOR PROTECTION

PROTECTION TOOLS CHART

The chart on the following two pages will help you identify days of the week, crystals, colors, herbs, and candles for quick reference when you are conducting spells or when you need protection.

DAY OF THE WEEK	MONDAY	TUESDAY	WEDNESDAY
CANDLES	Black	Blue	White
HERB	Basil	Frankincense	Myrrh
COLORS	Black	Blue	White
CRYSTAL	Apache tears	Tiger's-eye	Carnelian
PROTECTION	Protection for finances	Strength to fight against negative forces	Communication to solve altercations with negative people

THURSDAY	FRIDAY	SATURDAY	SUNDAY
Red	Blue and red	White and black	Yellow and black
Garlic	Dragon's blood	Rice	Rosemary
Red	Blue and red	White and black	Yellow and gold
Ruby	Red jasper	Aquamarine	Agate
Strengthen spirituality against negative forces	Protection against someone taking away a loved one	Fighting against negative forces	Protection against illness

CHART FOR GETTING RID OF NEGATIVITY

This chart can be used when you are in a hurry and don't have the time to do an actual spell. As long as you maintain positive visualization, you can accomplish your needs quickly and easily with this chart.

BAD SPIRITS	Light a black candle and a white candle and burn frankincense in the house on Saturdays and repeat again on Tuesdays.
NEGATIVE ENERGIES	To stop negative energies in their tracks, write down on a piece of paper the negativity you wish to end, stick it in a glass of water, and freeze it.
EVIL	In your censer, burn frankincense together with dragon's blood in the morning and at night to clear all types of evil.

GOSSIP	Write on a red cloth the name of the person who is spreading gossip, then fold the cloth and tape it together. Bury it under a dying plant and the gossip will end soon enough.
UN-HEXING	Add a tablespoon of salt, half a cup of coconut milk, half a teaspoon of olive oil, and a teaspoon of dry rue to a warm bath. Bathe in this mixture for seven nights.
PROTECTION FOR THE HOME	Keep a few old keys in a bowl behind the front door; then make an arrow out of cardboard. Write the protection needed by your home on the arrow and place it on top of the bowl facing the front door to keep anyone with bad intentions out of your home.
PROTECTION FOR YOUNG CHILDREN	Have young children carry or wear a tiger's-eye crystal and they will be protected.

PROTECTION OF FINANCES	Burn green candles in your place of employment and always have fresh basil around.
NEGATIVE MAGIC	Keep an apache tear crystal or a little red ribbon with you at all times to protect you or your loved ones from any negative workings. Wear black for protection, or wear red for strength against negative occult forces to reinforce your etheric body. You can also wear a pentagram pendant or visualize one over your chest every morning before you leave the house.

17

ONCE, TWICE, BUT NOT A THIRD TIME AROUND

I have deliberately divided up the spells in this book to suit the "strike me once, strike me twice, but never shall you strike me a third time around" method. This division will help you gauge the severity of your needs and deal with them accordingly, as there are things that can be fixed with simple spells and not lengthy rituals.

STRIKE ME ONCE—
THE WARNING: BE AWARE

The "strike me once" method is a quick-fix spell to ward away negative energies. This method could cover anyone from your boss giving you a hard time to the mother-in-law who never shuts up. It can also be used on entities and occult negative forces around you and in your home that you wish to expel. The "strike me once" method stops negative energies in mid-air. Like ice, they become frozen in time until they slowly fall to the ground without any direction or intent. It also serves as a warning signal for those sending negative energies that you are aware of their negative intentions.

STRIKE ME TWICE—
THE SECOND WARNING:
BE PREPARED

The "strike me twice" method should be used when you feel your first warning has failed. The message in strike me twice is to say "One more time and you're out!" This method will have a little bit more firepower and more tools will be used, such as candles or crystals.

NEVER A THIRD TIME—
THE THIRD WARNING: ACT UPON IT

This method is the final action. "Never a third time around" is used when the first two actions have failed, and people have suffered emotional or physical pain from negative forces like negative thought patterns or occult forces.

You will use the "third time around" action when there are hexes to be broken and curses to undo. This action is to be used only for when you have had enough of being the nice guy and you must stop the injustice aimed at you or your loved ones.

Long gone are the days when you needed to actually see someone to break a hex or help you with defensive magic. You can do it all yourself better than anyone else could. The key is to follow the rituals or the warning spells and to stay totally positive. Never say to yourself, "Did it work?" Instead, tell yourself, "It worked! I can feel it!" The spells are only there to keep you focused with the aid of natural energies that will manifest your needs. Your positive visualization sends these energies out into the universe with a bang, and you will never look back.

Stay focused, search your heart, and above all, make sure you are on the right track. Never blame the innocent—get your facts right before you do any of these spells; if uncertain, you can always do a protection spell with no names attached to it. In this way, the universe will find the person doing you wrong and direct the spell toward that person, ensuring that it's delivered to the one who is not in tune with the forces of nature.

18
SPELLS FOR THE "STRIKE ME ONCE" METHOD

THE WARNING: BE AWARE
BLUE LIGHT OF PROTECTION

Visualize a blue light around your home and family every morning. Doing so will protect your home from those who are sending negativity to your home.

KNOTS OF LOVE

Tie seven knots on a piece of rope. Then, dress a pink candle with lavender essential oil and the piece of rope. Light the candle and visualize peace to the one who wants war, and he or she will leave you alone.

HAIRY AND UGLY

If you keep a coconut behind your front door, no one can harm you with negative actions or thoughts.

LOCK THEM UP

A key tied with a blue bow behind the door will lock away unwelcome energies that are penetrating your home.

TRIANGLE TRAP

Fill three glasses with water, and then make sure they touch each other in a triangle formation. Place them where no one can touch them in order to protect your home from negative entities.

NOT TO BE SEEN

Wear a pair of red underpants inside-out to keep away the negative energies sent from people who wish to destroy your sex life.

BABY BE SAFE

Place a tiger's-eye and an apache tear crystal in a little blue bag and hang it inside your baby's crib or stroller to keep your baby safe and sound. Make sure it is out reach of the baby.

UNFORESEEN EVENTS

Don't find yourself unprotected from uncontrollable situations. Tie a blue, red, and white ribbon together and carry it with you at all times.

STINKY AND STICKY

Burn raw brown sugar on a charcoal tablet after unwanted visitors leave your home. This will be good for the well-being of your home.

FOUR CORNERS

Fill four bottle caps with household ammonia and place them in the four corners of your home. Doing so will keep your home safe and secure.

GOSSIP

Use a pin to write on a black candle the name of the person who is spreading harmful gossip. Place the candle in the freezer and the gossip will cease.

ABSORB IT

Before you go to bed at night, leave a glass of water where your family gets together to sit down, talk, and relax. In the morning when you wake up, take the glass outside and throw its contents onto your front lawn. All the negative energies from the day before will be absorbed into the water and will be gone.

CHAKRA PROTECTION

Get a meter (about three feet) each of red, orange, yellow, green, blue, purple, and pink ribbons. Make a braid out of the ribbons, then tie the braid around your waist to strength your chakras, so no one can mess with or weaken them.

RIGHT FOOT FORWARD

Every morning, leave the house with your right foot first. In doing so, no one can take away your right of way.

VAMP ZAP

Hang a bunch of garlic from your front door to keep away unwanted negative forces from your home. Don't use the garlic for cooking—that's not what it's there for!

REFLECTION

Always have a mirror facing your front door—it will reflect those negative thoughts from unwanted visitors back where they came from.

BLUE PEN

Tie a blue ribbon around the pen you use in order to protect your space from those who wish to ridicule your work.

CLEAR QUARTZ

Wear a clear quartz crystal to repel negative forces from penetrating your aura field.

ANGRY BOSS NO MORE

Sweeten up your boss by writing his or her name on a piece of paper and then pouring honey all over it. Leave the paper alone for a few days and you will see the change take place. Repeat again whenever needed.

PEACE AND QUIET

Light blue and white candles whenever you need to keep your home a peaceful haven.

ANOTHER FOUR-CORNER JOB

Get four clear quartz-point crystals and place them in the four corners of your home for protection against the forces outside your control.

PROTECTION SMOKE

Burn frankincense incense on Saturdays to keep your home clean from negative forces. Doing so will give such forces no choice but to get up and go.

HOWDY, NEIGHBOR

For a neighbor to be friendlier, mix dry thyme and white sugar in a bowl and sprinkle the mixture between both your homes. This will help you to get along better.

OH, NOT THE MOTHER-IN-LAW!

Light a pink candle and, before your mother-in-law arrives, recite out loud:

*"See no mess; smell no shame; the children are okay;
there is no need to speculate because you love us anyway."*

A THORN AT WORK

Mix together half a teaspoon of cumin powder and one teaspoon of dry angelica, and sprinkle them around the person's work station. Visualize this person getting along with others or finding another job.

FLICK AWAY

When you feel you have picked up negative vibes from someone, flick a white hanky all around you. The negative energies you picked up will go away as quickly as they came.

PROTECTION WITH CRYSTALS

No matter the crystal's shape or size, carry one with you at all times just in case—and you will forever be protected.

LIGHT ZAPPERS

As soon as you know that this person is coming, rub a little bit of frankincense essential oil in your hands. When this person enters your home, give them a big hug or a pat on the back. Doing so will prevent them from taking your energy away with them.

I WISH YOU TO LEAVE

Place a straw broom behind the front door with a touch of salt on the top. This will make the unwanted visitor think about their own home—and they will quickly leave yours.

ENTITIES BEGONE

Place as many garlic peels as you can on top of a charcoal tablet. The resulting smell will make any entities go away. (You can do the same with sulfur, but don't inhale; it's toxic!)

HATE GOSSIP?

Sprinkle salt around you and no gossip will ever come near you.

ROSEMARY

Wear a small branch of rosemary close to your heart and no emotional upset will enter your heart from others who wish you harm.

SWEET PROTECTION

Make a pentagram out of large or small cinnamon sticks, using copper wire to keep it all together. Hang the pentagram behind your front door and sweet protection will forever be in your home.

EVIL, EAT YOUR HEART OUT

Carry dill seeds in a little red drawstring bag to keep evil people away.

FRESH AS PINE

If one isn't already there, plant a pine tree outside your front door. It will protect your home all day while you are at work.

THEFT CONTROL

Place three old keys in a little red drawstring bag. Fill the bag with caraway seeds, and hang it above the front door. It will prevent people from taking what is yours.

BUNDLE OF PROTECTION

Tie three acorns together with a red ribbon and hang them outside your front door for protection from any negative forces wanting to invade your peaceful home.

SPIRITS BEGONE

Place a teaspoon of dry boneset and a tiger's-eye crystal inside a little blue drawstring bag. Carry it with you for protection against evil spirits.

THE BOGEYMAN

Place caraway seeds in a little dream pillow to protect the young from nightmares and from being scared.

CIRCLE IN THE MIDDLE

Make a small circle with pinecones, and in the middle place a teaspoon of asafetida. Draw a pentagram with your fingers on top. Doing so will protect you from negative occult forces.

19
SPELLS FOR THE "STRIKE ME TWICE" METHOD

THE SECOND WARNING: BE PREPARED
TO STOP AN ALTERCATION WITH NEIGHBORS

Light a yellow candle and burn benzoin essential oil in your oil burner. Fill a basket with ripe peaches. As you place each peach in the basket, visualize you and your neighbor actually being nice to each other. The next morning, leave the basket of peaches at the neighbor's front door and sneak back to your home. From that moment on, you will get a kind morning greeting and a smile from next door or across the road.

PROTECTION FOR AN INNOCENT SOUL

Mix a teaspoon of olive oil and half a teaspoon of dill seeds together on a Saturday, while thinking of the one that you seek protection for. Rub the mixture on a blue candle and embed as many dill seeds as you can into the candle. Write the name of the person you seek protection for on a piece of paper and place it under the candle—and then light the candle for about ten minutes. Light the same candle for ten minutes every day for seven days, always visualizing this person and wishing them no harm.

ASTRAL PROTECTION

Before astral traveling, light a white candle and ask your guide to direct and protect you against any harm in the astral world. Always hold a fresh clipping of rue, and then begin your travels with peace in mind. You will come to no harm from the ones who want to try and harm you.

BAD LUCK OUT THE DOOR

Light a white candle on a Saturday morning. While the candle burns, start cleaning your home. Use ammonia to clean the floors, and sprinkle rock salt over any carpeting. After all is clean and tidy, burn hawthorn berry, dry basil leaves, and two or three frankincense tears in your censer. Diffuse this smoke all over the house to leave good energies behind and to get rid of all the bad luck. Vacuum up the rock salt before noon on the following day.

NOT MY CHILD, YOU DON'T!

When your child leaves for school, open his or her bedroom window. Light one yellow candle and one red candle in the room. Doing so will give your child strength. Burn hyssop and sage together in your censer and take this sacred smoke into the room to help your child deal with peer pressure. Let the candles burn for a while and let the smoke linger so that the protection your child needs will keep.

ENVY ME NOT

Mix together a teaspoon of castor oil with seven peppercorns as you visualize the person who envies you so much. Dress a candle with the oil and embed the seven peppercorns within the candle. As you watch the candle being consumed, the person's envy will melt away, never to cause you pain again.

CLEARING THE SELF

Take the following items into your bathroom: a white candle, your censer with the charcoal already lit to burn, three frankincense tears (open the window as it will be very smoky), two white flowers, and an egg that has been out of the fridge for about an hour. Undress in privacy and place the censer on the floor by your feet. Pass the flowers all over your body, and do not stop until all the petals have landed on the floor. Open your arms and let the smoke engulf you, close your eyes, and visualize the wrongs leaving your soul and feel all the negativity others have placed on you as gone. Then hold the egg above your head and visualize it absorbing all the negativity in and around you. Next, run the egg all over your body—think of it as soap being used on a dry body. When you finish, crack the egg and flush it down the toilet. (Don't flush the eggshells though!)

SALT AND PEPPER

Draw a warm bath and add to the water one tablespoon of salt, a quarter teaspoon of black pepper, and a generous amount of dry rosemary. Light a white candle and a black candle and sit back and enjoy this magical bath. Make sure you wet your hair, as this bath will get rid of negative energies that have been sent purposely toward you. It will revitalize your aura and make your spirits high, ready to soar to the sky while negative energies become a thing of the past.

NOT MY PARTNER

Burn a rose incense stick and light a pink candle. While you do so, visualize your spouse or partner and how much you are in love with each other. Bring to mind the person trying to take your partner away from you, and place an imaginary stamp on this person's forehead and in your mind mail her or him all the way to Japan. Now visualize this person staying away from the one you love. Hold an Adam and Eve root and a carnelian crystal in your hand. Run them over the smoke from the incense and candle, thinking only of the one you love staying home. Place both the crystal and the root in a little red drawstring bag and place it under your partner's pillow. The lady or man friend who is after your partner will soon be packing up and going away.

REPEL EVIL AWAY

Place a block of camphor, a teaspoon of dry angelica, and some valerian and basil leaves in a kitchen pot you no longer use. Add four cups of water and bring the mixture to a boil. Carry your steaming pot around the house while chanting: *"Repel, repel evil away, never to be felt again."* You can do this whenever you feel the need to clear space.

CHILI PEPPERS TO GO, PLEASE!

Buy a dozen large chili peppers on a Tuesday (or even better, use homegrown ones if possible). Rub castor oil on each and every one of the peppers, making sure you wash your hands after doing so. You need a large blue cloth. A sheet also works well, as the fabric has to cover you up. Go out into the night, sit in your yard, and make a circle around you with the chili peppers. Then throw the blue cloth over yourself, visualizing all the evil gone and protection for your soul.

PROTECT YOUR BUSINESS

Make a cross out of two red pencils. Then light four green candles around the pencils and sprinkle Irish moss, yerba santa, and onion peels on top. Visualize the protection you seek for your business and from the one who wants you in the red. Do this on a Sunday and let the candles burn for about an hour.

TAKE HATRED AWAY FROM THE ONE WHO HATES

Make a heart-shaped pocket out of a red cotton cloth and place the name of the person who hates you inside it. Mix together rose petals, lemon peels, and catnip, and then add a few drops of vanilla essence. Stuff this mixture inside the heart-shaped pocket and sew the opening up. Light a pink candle while you visualize the hate leaving this person's heart, to be replaced with joy and happiness. Do this on a Wednesday and the hate will be gone.

STOP IN THE NAME OF LOVE

If someone is trying to take away the person you love, write the name of your loved one on a large piece of paper. Place some witch hazel and raw brown sugar on top of the name and wrap it all up. Tie the package with a red ribbon and place it under the bed of the one you love—this will keep the hands of the octopus away!

PEACE

As long as there is peace in the home, negative energies will not penetrate, since these energies require discord and arguments to feed from. If there is tension in your home, burn a few cooking cloves and fresh rosemary leaves on a charcoal tablet. You can do this anytime you want to keep your home at peace.

ONLY AT MY FRONT DOOR

To keep negative entities from entering your home, light a white candle outside your front door. Negative entities need light to grow and develop spiritually. A lit candle at your front doorstep helps the entities "get it," and they will see no need to come in to have a feast.

UP TO NO GOOD

Light a pink candle and a blue candle in the center of your altar while visualizing the negative force from which you need protection. Place a carnelian agate and an apache tear crystal in a black drawstring bag; then also place a High John the Conqueror root inside this little protection bag. Light a frankincense incense stick, run the bag over the smoke, and make a wish for all those up to no good to be gone, never to harm you as long as you carry this bag close to your heart. You can do this for anyone in need.

SUPER BANGER

Mix a half-teaspoon of blessed thistle, angelica, dragon's blood, frankincense, and myrrh together in your mortar and pestle. As you crush them together, visualize the entity you wish gone. Light a white candle and a blue candle; then start what I call the "Super Banger": burning the herbs together in your censer for maximum protection against negative entities in your home. Bring this smoke all over the house and chant:

"Go, go, begone and never return!"

WASH AWAY

Unfortunately, after you have a bad day at work, you can't help but bring into your home all the negative energies that have stuck to your aura field. When this happens, draw a warm bath and light a white candle in the bathroom. Add an entire tablespoon of vinegar, a cup of milk, and a cup of pineapple juice to the bath. Stay in this bath for about ten minutes and visualize all the worries of the day washing away. When you take out the plug, watch your bad day go down the drain.

PRISON DIRT

Sweep the dust and dirt from a prison's front door and take it home. Place the dirt in a little blue drawstring bag and make a note on parchment paper: "You will never harm me, because in prison you will be—the iron bars stopping you from ever harming me." Put this note in the drawstring bag and keep it with you at all times.

LIGHT OF PROTECTION

Half an hour before you go to work in the morning, light a blue candle and visualize the protection needed by your family and home. Then visualize the ones you love inside the candle's flame with a blue protection light around them. No one will ever harm them or intend to harm them, as the light of justice is on your side.

GET RID OF THE UGLY PAST TO MAKE THE FUTURE BRIGHT

Get rid of the wrongs imposed by others' evil eyes. Go back to the first time bad luck started to follow you around. Remember the date and write it down with a pin on a black candle. Now add a dash and write down the date on which you're conducting the spell. On a green candle, write the date of the spell with the same pin, followed once again by a dash, and then write the year 2099. Light the black candle first and visualize it consuming and melting all the wrongs you wish to rid yourself of, and then light the green candle. Visualize all that you wish to accomplish in this lifetime, with only good luck from the date of this spell until 2099. Both candles must consume all the way to the end. The spell will then start working for the end of bad luck and for good luck to come your way.

ABUSE NOT MY HOSPITALITY

If someone visits every day at a certain time and stays too long, write their name on a piece of parchment paper along with the following: "When you come to visit, please don't stay long. You are needed in your own home." Fold the paper nice and tight and place it inside a toy vehicle that looks like the car your visitor drives or the bus he or she takes to get to your home. Place the toy car or bus close to your front door ready to drive away.

THE DEATH CARD

Light two blue candles on your altar and place the Death card from a tarot deck between the candles. Place an anise star on top of the card and then sit back and visualize the end of what is bothering you or the person you wish to stop bothering you. See the mysterious horseman on the Death card moving across your troubled path and taking with him everything that interferes in your life. Let the candles burn down halfway, and then relight them the next day until they reach their end. Discard the anise star in a place where there will never be any growth, but will see rebirth.

PSYCHIC PROTECTION POT

Place a cup of water, a teaspoon of blue food dye, one teaspoon of wood betony, and a carnelian agate crystal inside an old pot that you no longer cook with. Bring all this to a boil. When it steams, carry it all over the house. Doing so will protect you from unexpected psychic attacks and sudden negative energies that could make the hairs on the back of your neck stand on end.

LET'S GET ALONG BETTER TOGETHER

Would you like to make amends and improve a situation for everyone's sake? Sprinkle coriander around the person you want to get along with—you can even sprinkle it on the person's front door—and you will start to get along better. With business rivals, rub your hands with coriander before shaking their hands—and you will have a better understanding of each other's business and what your rivals want.

FOR UNSTABLE MINDS

Mix crushed dry rosemary leaves with two drops of marjoram oil until a paste is made. Then rub the whole mixture on a pink candle. Write on the candle the name of the person who is unknowingly causing harm to everyone with whom he or she makes contact and whose negative energies you want to stabilize. Patience is required as these people suffer from mental illness. They do not consciously mean you harm, but both protection and awareness are needed in order to understand them.

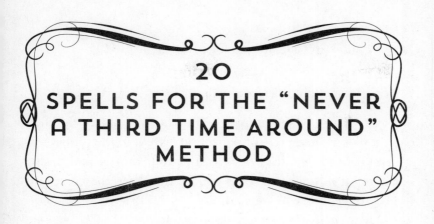

20
SPELLS FOR THE "NEVER A THIRD TIME AROUND" METHOD

THE THIRD WARNING: ACT UPON IT
TO REMOVE A CURSE

This spell will remove curses placed before your time by ancestors. You can also use it for more recent curses and for friends who have been cursed for someone's self gain. You can also do this ritual to exorcise unwanted entities from a corporal being.

You will need:

- Eggshell of 1 egg
- 2 blue candles (dress with castor oil)
- 1 black candle (dress with castor oil)

- 1 barbecue charcoal
- Censer and a charcoal tablet
- 1 teaspoon of angelica
- 1 teaspoon of blessed thistle

Crack an egg and empty its contents; then place the shell on top of a white piece of paper and leave it in the sunlight to dry. Once dry, crush the eggshell in your mortar and pestle, making it into a powder. As you do this, keep the curse you wish to terminate in your mind.

On a Tuesday when the moon is waning, light the two blue candles and visualize what you wish to be gone. Then light the black candle while visualizing the hurt this curse has caused. See the curse being consumed by the flame of the candle. Place the black candle between the blue candles.

With the barbecue charcoal, draw a pentagram on your forehead and a pentagram on your chest, visualizing the pentagrams drawing out the curse that was placed upon your physical and spiritual self.

Mix the angelica and the blessed thistle and start burning the mixture in your censer. Next, anoint your forehead and chest with the powder of the crushed eggshell. As you do so, say:

*"Evil that was placed upon me shall no longer exist.
YOU will terminate this day and leave this sacred site,
my body, and my life."*

Stop for a moment and focus completely on the words you are speaking. See all the wrongdoing leave your body like a suction cup; when you feel it leave, say with strength:

*"STAY AWAY . . . BE GONE
for the good of my soul and all!"*

With the eggshell powder, draw a circle around the black candle and then quickly extinguish the candle with your right index finger. Follow this by immediately breaking the black candle in half, visualizing all that was done to you breaking apart in front of your eyes. Take the candle and bury it deep in a place where you know it will never surface again. From this date forward, you will be your old self again.

PROTECTION USING THE CHAKRAS

Using the chakras, you can protect against both enemies and negative energies that want to emotionally or physically weaken you and those you love. This is an excellent spell to use for individuals who have been physically or verbally abused. It should give such people the strength they need to make the abuse stop. If you are using this spell for such a purpose, visualize the abused person's needs and see her or him as you go through each chakra in the spell. Place the abused person's name under the white candle.

You will need:

- 1 white candle (dress with marjoram essential oil)
- 1 of each of the following candles: red, orange, yellow, green, blue, purple, pink (dress with corn oil)
- A bunch of eucalyptus leaves
- 1 teaspoon of fennel
- 1 teaspoon of sage
- 7 sunflower seeds
- 1 meter (about three feet) of red ribbon
- 1 small piece of paper

Mix the fennel and the sage together in your mortar and pestle on a Sunday when the moon is either full or nearly full; then burn the mixture in your censer one bit at a time. Light the white candle and visualize the one from whom you are defending yourself. Write your name, or the name of the person you are helping, on the piece of paper and place it under the candle. Then light all the other candles. Each color represents one of your chakras and its representative color, and you must therefore visualize what each color represents as follows:

- *Red:* Visualize the root chakra, the center of your emotions, stronger than ever before.
- *Orange:* Visualize the abdominal chakra nursing lovingly your relationships with loved ones, making those relationships strong and bonding.
- *Yellow:* Visualize the solar plexus, your gut feeling, never being wrong.
- *Green:* Visualize the heart chakra, your heart center, strong with all past issues resolved.
- *Purple:* Visualize the third eye, your psychic powers, expanding so you can see who is doing your soul wrong.
- *Pink:* Visualize the crown chakra, your spirituality, growing and understanding the faults of others.

Visualize a rainbow with these colors around you. See them like swirls never breaking the circle. Once all the candles are lit, put them into a circle with the white candle in the middle.

Visualize the white candle's flame engulfing your etheric field and the gold wings of angels lovingly around you. Say:

"From those who wish me harm
I will be [or: You will be] forever protected.
I have the gold wings of angels on my side
And they embrace me with protection
Fight me not, for it is you the
Golden army will be after."

Sprinkle the sunflower seeds and the eucalyptus leaves in the center of the circle. Visualize yourself in the center with protection all around you, ready to defend and ward away anything negative floating above you that has your name on it.

Let the candles burn down halfway, and then snuff them out. Gather all the candles together in a bunch, making sure the white one remains in the middle with the piece of paper attached. Wrap the red ribbon as many times as you can around all the candles. Place the bundle somewhere where it cannot be seen, but close enough for you to feel its protective peace.

PROTECTION AGAINST A SPECIFIC PERSON

You can do this spell anytime that you want protection for yourself or your home against a specific individual. It's also great to make a protection bottle to give to a friend who is in need of protection or, by visualizing the protection they seek as you make it, to make one for your partner or your child for their own protection.

You will need:

- 1 blue candle (dress with castor oil)
- 1 red candle (dress with castor oil)
- 1 teaspoon of hyssop
- 1 teaspoon of mistletoe
- 1 large pinch of salt
- Mortar and pestle
- Censer
- 1 blue cloth
- 1 small, shallow white or clear plate
- 1 small blue spray bottle
- 100 mL (just under ½ cup) of distilled water
- 5 drops of rosemary oil

Light both candles, visualizing the protection you seek. Mix the hyssop and mistletoe together in a mortar and pestle until it forms into a powder. While you're doing this, say over and over again the name of the person and the protection you seek, and then blend in the salt.

Once you're finished, place the protection powder you've made in the small plate and leave it between the candles. Then burn a pinch of the powder in your censer and let the smoke engulf the room. When the smoke ends, let the candles burn down right to the end.

The following morning, pick up the remaining powder and place it in the blue spray bottle. Fill the bottle with 100 mL of distilled water and five drops of rosemary essential oil. Shake the bottle gently before covering it with a blue cloth. Leave the covered bottle out in the moonlight and sunlight for three days and three nights.

No harm will be inflicted when you use this protection spray whenever you are around the person from whom you are seeking protection. You can also do this spell for anyone else in need of protection, or make a protection spray for your home.

PROTECT A STUFFED ANIMAL
FOR YOUR CHILD

This spell is for children—either your own children or a friend's children—who are having difficulties adjusting to "lights out" or who see things in their bedroom that frighten them. These children can use this magical toy as their protector.

You will need:

- 1 orange candle (dress with baby oil)
- 1 red candle (dress with olive oil)
- 1 emerald crystal
- Censer
- 1 teaspoon of yarrow
- 1 teaspoon of basil
- 1 tablespoon of rice
- 1 stuffed animal your child likes and can identify with, such as a bear, tiger, lion, or dog

Light both candles and visualize the protection your child needs or that which scares your child. The protection needed could be from bad dreams, the bogeyman, or the kid down the street who bullies your child.

Burn the yarrow in your censer and run the smoke over the emerald crystal, then over the basil and the rice. Keep the smoke going at any cost. Now make a small incision on the stuffed animal, close to where you think its heart is, remove some of the stuffing, and place the emerald crystal, the yarrow, the basil, and the rice inside the stuffed animal's newfound heart.

Move the stuffed toy over the smoke while you say:

*"Go forth and protect my child from
dreams or anything in between;
the keeper of the key to my child's safety you will be."*

Then sew up the cut and say:

*"Suffer not, be scared not, my child,
for this toy animal will protect you from harm."*

As you're doing this, visualize the stuffed animal coming to life and sitting at the bedside of the child, with its majestic sight scaring away anyone who wishes your child harm. Leave the new keeper of your child's safety next to the candles for a while. Then give this stuffed animal to your child as a present.

Ask the child to name the new toy and to whisper its name in your ear. The new toy's name should only be known to you both, and the name used only when your child is in need and calls it out for protection.

PROTECTION AGAINST SOMEONE STEALING YOUR ESSENCE

This is a very powerful spell that can be used for just about any type of situation in which you feel negative energies or forces are trying to get the better of you.

You will need:

- 2 blue candles (dress with frankincense essential oil)
- 1 gold candle (dress with frankincense essential oil)
- 1 black silk square cloth
- ¼ teaspoon of dragon's blood
- 4 frankincense tears
- Small pair of scissors
- 1 teaspoon of salt
- 1 teaspoon of ague weed
- 1 meter (about three feet) of red ribbon
- 1 small pinecone

On a waning moon, preferably on a Saturday night, light the two blue candles while visualizing a blue light of protection around you. Light the gold candle and visualize gold rings, like bands of steel, that hum and repel anyone who tries to do you harm.

Spread the black cloth on your altar table, then start to burn the dragon's blood and the frankincense tears in your censer. Cut a small lock of your hair with the scissors and say:

"Lock of my hair, core of my existence."

Gently place the lock of hair on top of the black cloth. Cut the nails of your right hand (if you are left-handed, then cut the nails of your left hand) and say:

> *"Nails, essence of my existence,*
> *secure and hold this lock and*
> *like cats' claws you will protect it*
> *and never leave it unattended."*

Place your nail clippings on top of your lock of hair, and then hold the salt in both of your hands. Rub your hands together, letting the salt fall on top of the cloth, while you say:

> *"My essences are mine and only mine*
> *And not for anyone to play or manipulate me with them."*

Now sprinkle the ague weed on top, making sure nothing spills. Make a bundle of the cloth, then tie the red ribbon around the bundle as many times as you can. As you do this, say over and over again:

> *"Curse me not with my essence,*
> *locked away they are and shall remain,*
> *never to be reached by any negative forces*
> *wanting to have them."*

Let the candles consume, and keep the black cloth in a place no one knows about but you.

SENDING IT BACK TO NEGATIVE FORCES

This spell is a quick way to send back whatever has been sent to you. You are not doing a spell to pay someone back. You are simply sending back the hurt another has caused you—and that person will feel it.

You will need:

- 2 white candles (dress with olive oil)
- 1 pink candle (dress with baby oil)
- ¼ teaspoon of myrrh
- 1 teaspoon of castor oil
- 1 teaspoon of honey
- 1 teaspoon of damiana
- 1 small rubber ball
- 1 small white plate

On a Sunday when you are at peace and on your own, light the white candles with only thoughts in mind of the person who has done you harm and what that harm has done to you and your life.

Burn the myrrh in your censer to seek protection for yourself against the one who likes to inflict pain. Then mix the castor oil, the honey, and the damiana together on a small white plate. As you mix this all together, bring this person to mind and keep that thought in your mind. As you anoint the rubber ball with everything on the plate, say:

> *"May your own words and actions bite you back,*
> *to never harm an innocent soul when around.*

Be it for good, a lesson you will learn by
taking back your desired intent."

Hold the rubber ball in your right hand, as tight as your grip will allow. Visualize all the pain you have suffered and imagine it going inside the ball. Once you know the ball holds everything you don't want, take it to the front of the home of the one who has wished you wrong and say:

"Back to where you came from you must go
I wish no longer to play your game.
Return to the one you belong
and take with you the hurt you have caused."

Then throw the rubber ball as far as you can and you will never again play with those who don't play fair with universal games. If you don't know where this individual resides, just take the ball to the sea or a nearby creek and throw it as far as you can, and it will be express-delivered by the water element on your behalf.

TO FIND WHO IS DOING YOU WRONG

You can do this spell when you know someone is out there sending you negative energies, but you don't know who it may

255

be. This spell will aid you in identifying the source, which you can then deal with accordingly.

You will need:

- 3 drops of rosemary essential oil
- 2 drops of frankincense essential oil
- 1 red candle, 1 blue candle, 1 green candle, 1 yellow candle, and 2 white candles (dress all the candles with olive oil)
- 1 teaspoon of black pepper
- 1 map of your local area

On a Wednesday, start your oil burner and blend in both of the essential oils. Open your local map and spread it out on a table or your altar, depending on the size of the map. As you're doing this, focus on your will to find the person who is getting away with the injustice in your life. Follow this by lighting the white candles and placing them on top of the middle of the map. Say:

"Guardians of light, focus on the person I wish to find."

Light the red candle and place it on top of the map where south is, and say:

*"Element of fire, be my strength and walk late at night
to find the person wishing me harm."*

Light the blue candle and place it on top of the map where west is and say:

*"Element of water travel over sea, lakes and rivers of
this town and find the person wishing me harm."*

Light the yellow candle and place it on top of the map where east is and say:

*"Element of air give me the intuition to know
and find the person wishing me harm."*

Finally, light the green candle and place it on top of the map where north is and say:

*"Element of the earth, travel the hills and the plains of this town
and help me find the person wishing me harm."*

Sprinkle the pepper on top of the map and say:

"You, the one in the shadows
who likes to hide in the dark,
come forth and identify yourself
and let's get this masquerade out of the way."

Visualize this person coming forth and ask your guides to aid you in identifying this person behind the mask. Let the candles consume all the way to the end and leave the map out as the elements are still working on the task you have set. You will know who the person is, and then protection you shall seek.

GETTING RID OF UNWANTED ENTITIES SENT TO DISTURB YOU AND YOUR HOME

To do their bidding, some negative forces seek out souls that are lost. These souls are unaware of their circumstances and quite possibly were corrupted during their physical lives. This spell will help these lost souls find light, leave your home, and continue their spiritual journeys.

You will need:

- 2 white candles (dress with olive oil)
- 1 green candle (dress with olive oil)
- 1 yellow candle (dress with olive oil)

- Censer
- A bunch of dry garlic peels
- A pinch of sulfur (make sure that you do NOT inhale the smoke; protect yourself accordingly!)
- ¼ teaspoon of dragon's blood
- 1 small bowl of water

On a Tuesday when the moon is full, light the white candles with visions of the entity you wish were out of your home. Then light the green candle and wish this entity the spiritual growth necessary to cross over. Next, light the yellow candle to bring understanding to the entity, letting it know it is time to leave you and your home alone and to go to the next stage of its spiritual journey.

Add the garlic peels on top of the charcoal tablet that is already burning in the censer. Add the dragon's blood. While the smoke circles around the candles, say:

> *"Go spirit of the night.*
> *Find the light; enough is enough:*
> *Leave us this night.*

Thou shall not return, as you will find
peace on the other side."

Add the sulfur. Stand away from the smoke, and say with strength:

"Tormented you will no longer be
and no longer will you do another's dirty deeds.
Go, go, go—and get out of my home!"

Take the smoke around your home and chant the above over and over again. Start from the back of the house and finish at your front door. Repeat every day during the full moon, and again if the negative entity ever comes back to bother you.

BRINGING A PARTNER BACK

This spell can help to make a partner who has left think about you and the love you once shared. It will light a spark that will override negative forces and let in what was once real love.

You will need:

- Oil burner
- 3 drops of rose oil essential with jojoba
- 2 drops of ylang-ylang essential oil

- 2 pink candles (dress with baby oil)
- The person's astral color candle (dress with olive oil)
- Your astral color candle (dress with olive oil)
- A photograph of both of you during happy times
- ½ meter (just over 1½ feet) of pink ribbon
- 1 pinch of cinnamon powder

Mix the rose and the ylang-ylang oils in your oil burner on a Friday night, with thoughts in your mind about why your other half left. Then light the pink candles, while thinking about your love and that which you two shared and enjoyed doing together. Place the photo in the middle of the pink candles, light the person's astral color candle, and say:

"Think of the good times we had
and the caring things said;
truly search your heart
and light the fire again in your heart."

Then light your astral color candle and say:

"If there is still love, come back to me!
If there is still trust, come back to me!

261

If you are under a spell, think back;
Open your heart and let me back inside."

Roll the photo into the shape of a scroll and lightly tie a bow around it with the pink ribbon. Bring both astral color candles together, nearly touching, and place the photo scroll in front of them. Let it sit there until all the candles are consumed to the very end. Keep the scroll in a safe place.

Always remember that love is not to be manipulated. If it was stolen without any magic, then it wanted to be stolen! If it wasn't, the love will come back—as those types of negative spells only last for a short while. Protect your love and it will be always yours.

NOT TO SEEK REVENGE

We have no right to seek revenge no matter how sweet we may think it will be. Karma will seek it for you in other ways. But you do need to protect yourself from the infliction of negative forces.

You will need:

- 2 white candles (dress with baby oil)
- 1 black candle (dress with patchouli oil)

- 1 pink candle (dress with rose oil)
- 1 amethyst crystal
- 1 teaspoon of chamomile
- Censer and charcoal

When the moon is waxing, light both of the white candles with thoughts of peace to your soul whenever it is troubled and does not know which way to go. Burn the chamomile in your censer, and let its scent calm and purify you. Feel the peace and comfort only chamomile can bring.

Follow this by lighting the black candle. As you do, feel all the anger you have toward a specific individual or the situation that is making you want to seek revenge. Feel your anger burning away and say:

> *"Revenge feels sweet but is not for me;*
> *there are other ways to seek justice*
> *and revenge is not it."*

Light the pink candle and see anger replaced with love. Say:

> *"I am a child of the universe and*
> *a faithful member I have been.*

263

> *I will not tarnish it for something such as this.*
> *Revenge I will not seek*
> *but protection I seek against the ills placed upon me."*

Feel peace and understanding, the anger already a thing of the past. Seek not to harm but to receive protection. Let the candle consume, and do a protection spell or the "Sending It Back to Negative Forces" spell earlier in this chapter.

RESTORE THE MARRIAGE STOLEN

You can do this spell if you feel your marriage or relationship with a longtime partner has come—or is coming—to an end, and you believe negative forces are part of the reason. This spell will help your partner to see the wrongs done and start fresh once again if it's meant to be.

You will need:

- Both of your astral color candles
- 1 wedding photograph (or a photo of you both together)
- 2 gold rings (it's just a symbol, so toy rings are okay)
- ½ meter (just over 1½ feet) of pink and red ribbon
- 2 teaspoons of rose water

- 1 small blue drawstring bag
- ½ teaspoon of dry yarrow
- 1 pink candle (dress with lavender essential oil)
- 1 green candle (dress with marjoram essential oil)

On a Friday night when the moon is full, place both astral color candles on top of the wedding photo. Visualize the love you had and the love you shared, which is timeless and only you could understand and bear. Look at the photo and wish yourself once again there.

Place the two gold rings in a small bowl containing the rose water. This will bring back the marriage that has been taken away.

Light the pink candle and silently ask your love if he or she feels the same way, and to search his or her heart to see if the fire still burns and to feel the love once again that was. When you light the green candle, see the love that was once there growing and never-ending, and say:

> *"Like it was before, it will be again*
> *to its original state;*
> *if it's mine to keep, it will be."*

Let the candle consume for about ten minutes. Continue thinking of love and its return by visualizing the person to blame not wanting your partner's love anymore. While the candles are still sending your message to the universe, fold the photo as small as you can get it. Then place it inside the blue drawstring bag, adding the yarrow. Take the rings out of the rose water and wrap the red and pink ribbons around them. While you are doing this, say over and over again:

> *"To have and to love, from this day forward;*
> *if under a spell it is now broken*
> *and my love will return home shortly."*

Keep the drawstring bag with you during the day and under your pillow at night.

STAY AWAY, MY ENEMY

You can do this spell when you feel all the other spells using the earlier methods have failed and enough is enough.

You will need:

- 2 blue candles (dress with marjoram essential oil)
- 1 red candle (dress with marjoram essential oil)

- 1 small glass jar
- ½ cup of vinegar
- 1 teaspoon of blue food dye
- 1 egg white
- 1 peppercorn
- 1 pinch of dry mulberry leaves
- 1 small piece of parchment paper

Light the blue candles on a Tuesday when there is no moon, and think of your enemies and the reason why you wish them to stop and be gone. Light the red candle for strength and to tell your enemies you are not as soft as they thought you were, and say:

> *"Enemy you are and enemy you will no longer be because you will no longer be able to bother me."*

Place the vinegar, the blue food dye, the egg white, the peppercorn, and the dry mulberry leaves in the jar, and say:

> *"A bad taste in your mouth you will have when you mention my name."*

Write the name of those who want to harm you—and your wish for them to stay at arm's length—on the piece of parchment paper. Place the parchment paper inside the jar and close it. Then, with your right hand, hold the jar and shake it, making the contents go around and around. Say:

> *"Here you go around the mulberry bush,*
> *and you will keep going around until*
> *you stop harassing me for reasons I can't figure out."*

Once a day for seven days, vigorously shake the contents of the jar and say the above over and over again, and your enemy or enemies will stay away.

21
SPELLS FOR SELF-INFLICTED CURSES

THE SPELLS
BANISH DEPRESSION

Depression varies from person to person and is, at times, triggered by emotional upsets encountered in daily life. If you find that you lack motivation or are frequently sad or even overly irritable, you may be suffering from depression. By conducting this very simple spell, you will once again feel in control to banish depression every time you feel it coming.

You will need:

- 1 red candle
- 1 red jasper crystal (cleanse with rainwater and leave it out in the sunlight for a day)

Light the red candle as you visualize your depression being replaced by newfound inner strength, and say:

"Strength I have and inner love I have found;
depression does no longer have a place in my life."

Carry the red jasper with you at all times to fight the depression bug and always light a red candle when depressed.

CONQUERING FEAR

Fear comes from the discomfort in situations you don't want to face. Search within and find the root of the fear that is stopping you from moving forward. Remember: fear is what you perceive it to be and not what it really is. Face the demons you carry and confront them so you don't have to deal with them again.

You will need:

- 1 wire coat hanger
- 1 letter-size (or A4-size) piece of parchment paper
- 2 clothes pegs
- 1 sink full of water mixed with 1 teaspoon of bleach

On the piece of paper, write down the fear you want to conquer and how you hope to conquer it. Then dip the paper in the sink and let it soak there for a while. Using the two clothes pegs, hang the paper on the coat hanger and leave it there to dry as you say:

"My deepest fear, out of my heart, I hang you out to dry, once and for all out of my life."

Remove the paper from the sink. Once it is dry, burn it and take the ashes to a hill. Bury the ashes there to rest in peace.

FINDING A SOLUTION TO A PROBLEM

You will avoid daily stressors if you deal with your problems before they get out of control. Ask your guide for help and guidance for a speedy solution to your pending problem.

You will need:

- 2 white candles
- 1 bunch of white flowers
- 3 drops of lavender essential oil on your oil burner

Light both candles and place the bunch of white flowers between them. Burn lavender oil in your oil burner. Sit down and relax, thinking of your spiritual guide; he is the one that knows the troubles of your heart. In a completely meditative state, ask your guide to aid you with the problem at hand and to give you a solution that will satisfy you. You will have your answer—if not right away, then within a few days.

GAINING SELF-CONFIDENCE

By gaining confidence, your mind sets out on a quest to satisfy the soul. Once accomplished, there is a newfound assurance that feeds and satisfies the soul, which will enable you to trust the decisions you make.

You will need:

- 1 red drawstring bag
- 3 acorns
- 1 teaspoon of saffron

Take the little red drawstring bag and place the three acorns and the teaspoon of saffron inside. Leave the bag out in the sunlight for three hours, and then hold it in your hand and feel the energy it now has. Feed from it to gain the confidence you wish to have.

IMPROVE YOUR LOST SELF-WORTH

When you lose your sense of self-worth, your entire existence feels fabricated. You don't trust or believe in yourself. By building your self-worth up to where it once was, you can start to believe in and trust yourself again.

You will need:

- 1 old photograph of yourself
- 1 old piece of clothing you once wore and felt secure in
- 1 white candle (dress with sandalwood essential oil)
- 1 yellow candle (dress with sandalwood essential oil)
- 1 green candle (dress with sandalwood essential oil)

Place the photo of yourself on top of your piece of clothing and, one by one, light the candles around them both. Sit quietly and visualize the person you once were and would like to be again. Feel that energy once more; feed from the lost strength and start liking yourself. Let the candles consume right to the very end. Then place the piece of clothing and the photo under your mattress—and you will once again be filled with self-worth.

OVERCOME ENVY

Once you are able to let go of envy, you will find that you will no longer place images of others or what they have in your mind. Be happy with what you have—it could be worse and you could have less than you do; that is true for all things physical and material.

You will need:

• 1 green candle

Light a green candle every day for seven days, always visualizing your envy burning away and leaving the core of your soul pink and full of love.

QUIET YOUR NERVES

We all need a time out to calm and relax the soul. Your nerves can get the better of you. By knowing how to relax, you will be able to calm your nerves.

You will need:

- 3 candles—1 pink, 1 white, 1 yellow
- 3 drops of ylang-ylang essential oil
- 4 drops of lavender essential oil
- 1 fresh white flower
- ½ cup of coconut milk
- 1 tablespoon of olive oil

Draw a warm bath and light all the candles around the bathroom. Add the oils, flower, coconut milk, and olive oil to the bath. Turn down the lights and enjoy this soothing bath—your nerves will go and you will feel as never before. You can have this bath anytime you feel the need to settle down your nerves.

RELIEVE GUILT

You know you have a conscience when you feel guilt and blame yourself for actions you wish you could retract. By doing the following, you will think before you act and know when not to feel guilty for actions that have been done.

You will need:

- 1 aventurine crystal (cleansed with rainwater)

Carry this crystal with you at all times; it will help you think before you act and you won't need to feel guilty for the things you've done, and for the future events to come.

STOP OVEREATING OR DRINKING

Overeating or drinking too much are signs that the physical self is not satisfied and is compensating in order to feel satisfied. Yet the feeling of satisfaction only lasts a short while—and many people find themselves overeating or drinking too much all over again. This spell will help you feel less hungry or lose the desire for more than one drink.

You will need:

- 3 almonds
- 1 teaspoon of catnip
- 1 blue drawstring bag

Place the almonds and the catnip inside the blue drawstring bag, and then hold the bag in your hand. Visualize what it is that your physical self is starving for. Carry this drawstring bag with you all the time and your hunger will no longer be for food or drink, but for life and love and whatever else your physical self craves.

TO HAVE MENTAL STABILITY

Do this spell when you feel your mind needs stability or a rest.

You will need:

- 1 white candle
- 2 drops of rosemary essential oil
- 3 drops of sandalwood essential oil

Light the candle and burn the essential oils in your oil burner whenever your mind is in turmoil and you have a need to feel mentally stable. You can also do this spell in someone's name for their particular mental stability needs.

IMPROVE SELF-ESTEEM

The best way to feel good about yourself is to build your self-esteem.

You will need:

- 1 rose quartz
- 1 drop of lavender essential oil
- 1 pink candle
- 1 small pink ribbon
- 1 pink drawstring bag

After cleansing the rose quartz crystal with the lavender oil, light the pink candle and feel its loving energy, like a ball penetrating the core of your soul. Make a bow out of the pink ribbon and place both the crystal and the bow inside the pink drawstring bag. Doing so will bring love to your soul and make you feel good about who you are. It will also aid you in accomplishing the things you want to accomplish in order to bring new worth and self-esteem to your life.

CLOSING

Curses are out there, and so are negative individuals, negative forces, and negative entities. They come in only if you let them, so don't let them come in. Stay mentally and physically strong. The more you acknowledge these negative forces, the more they will penetrate your spiritual and physical body for the simple reason that you are feeding them by making a big deal out of them. When you do that, you end up letting them win and achieve what they set out to do.

If you want to be treated fairly, then treat others as you wish to be treated. Don't let your ego win. If you do, you will lose the fight before it even starts. Negativity in some individuals can be contagious and hazardous to your health and spiritual growth, so try to stay away from negative people. Always try to say things in an affirmative manner. Never say, "I can't." Instead, say, "I can." Doing so will make achievable goals that you thought were unachievable.

Just as people can send negative thoughts, so they can send positive thoughts. If you have a dream, reach out for it and don't let anyone hold you back. No matter what they are, visualize your dreams to the universe. If you do so, you will see what can happen when you connect your positive thoughts and attitudes with the universe.

The universe and karma are always at your side, so don't worry about the wrongdoing of others. One day, justice will be achieved.

Blessed be,
Ileana

☆
WHITE
SPELLS

ON THE GO

INTRODUCTION

Ritual and magic governed every step, every thought, and every action of our ancestors' lives. Theirs was a time of worship, a time when festive seasons were named and celebrated according to planting and harvesting. But today, centuries later, ritual magic is long past its original heyday, and festivals are practiced symbolically by a faithful few. Yet there is something that lingers from ancestral generations, which is what I call "the essence": the essence of each individual family.

Each generation brings something sacred to the next: be it that secret recipe no one knows about, the blue eyes of your great-grandparents, the curly hair from your mother's side of the family, or the mannerisms of one of your parents. Not to mention your grandmother's advice, which I know you've taken or will someday take. I know I have, but mine was more on the magical, mystical side of things . . .

My family's generation gave me Santería, which is well known for its remedies. The smell of a lit cigar and the pungent, refreshing smell of Agua de Florida will always remind me of my youth, when I watched my father's guide, Francisco, give spiritual advice and counsel to my father's many clients with quick remedies.

I respect and hold Santería close to my heart, but I also love my Wiccan ways, so I combined Santería's remedies with my Wiccan beliefs and have created spells "on the go." Spells on the go are mini-spells that use earthbound energies to cause an effect without a lengthy ritual. Earthbound energies can be anything from a crystal, an herb, or the flame of a candle, to the water from a stream, the earth on the ground, or the air that brushes through the meadows and fields.

I am compelled to share in this book my most intimate spells on the go, which I have used with positive results over the years. I have also shared them with others who sought my advice and guidance, only to be informed later of their own encouraging results. When I'm short on cash, I light a green candle. When I feel the negative energy of an unwanted entity, I burn frankincense incense in the house. When I need my partner to help me around the house—well, I just engrave his name with a pin on a red candle and light it, and I can assure you that this gets him off the couch. And if there is a time when I feel my guide is not by my side, I light a white candle and say, "Hey, come back here! I need you."

We live in a world of quick fixes. There is always a quick fix for something—a quick coffee, a quick bite to eat. Fast-food restaurants are first on our list for quick fixes; we even go to drive-through bank tellers because doing so is quicker than stopping and parking the car to make a deposit or a withdrawal.

We hardly have time for ourselves, much less our family or friends. We seem to make appointments left, right, and center just to catch up, go to dinner, or merely get together.

Most of us no longer experience the personal touch of a handwritten letter, but rather we receive cold e-mails on white-and-gray screens. With Internet dating, I guess love letters are a thing of the past, too. An impersonal text message can bring news of a job, a birth, or even a death. The intimate touch that once existed is long gone, now that "www" has come into our world.

Time is not going to stop for us, no matter how much we want it to slow down. We need to keep up with the fast pace of life in our magical workings, and we can achieve this with quick magical fixes for our everyday needs, using natural earthbound energies. I can honestly say you'll never look back.

There is no ritual behind spells on the go, but they do have visualizations; I can assure you that a positive visualization can make the universe do wonders. The universe knows the fast pace we all live in, and it allows that fast pace in our magical workings, as does the Goddess. She always hears our cries for help—and if they're urgent, she's not going to say, "Hey, you need to do a ritual to dial my number," but instead she will say, "Let me see what I can do for you. I know you are in need."

By combining generations of magical know-how from Santería and Witchcraft, *spells on the go* are the only *way to go* in our fast-paced society. If we need to keep up to date with technology so that it doesn't pass us by, we need to do the same thing with magic. We cannot let generations of know-how pass into the history books just because there is no time for rituals. That is why, for anyone who wants to tap into magic, spells on the go are such a fresh concept.

Universal forces are always around us, and they are ready to listen to and act upon our desires and needs. You just need to make that connection with them—which might entail something as simple as lighting a white candle in order to take your message to the universe with the message "I need your help this day."

Have fun and enjoy *White Spells on the Go*, a book of spells for the modern world.

Blessed be,
Ileana

22
EARTHBOUND AND UNIVERSAL ENERGIES

Earthbound energies take your message to the universe. They are not hard to find because they are all around us. You can touch them, feel them, smell them, and even hold them; you can bring earthbound energies into your world to manifest your deepest dreams and desires. These energies are anything that are nourished and grown by nature, such as herbs, crystals, and more.

Apart from earthbound energies, there is also a universal energy. Universal energy is of course the universe, and within the universe there are other energies, including the planets, the moon, the sun, the stars, and the homes of our most beloved deities and guides.

When both universal and earthbound energies are brought together to cause an effect, the impact is mind-boggling and the possibility of manifestation is endless. This is what I call "the birth of magic."

Most people associate magic with the occult; this is because magic is part of wizardry, fantasy, and is on the mystical and mythical side of things. But the good thing about magic is that it is interpreted in many different ways; religious faith and beliefs don't even come close. Magic is inexplicable, and to try to analyze or make sense of it is absolutely futile. So why try to make sense of it? Just accept it—once you do, you immediately believe that the unavailable is accessible. And who doesn't want that?

Believing is the key to receiving anything we want, and once you let earthly and universal energies into your everyday life, you will be opening the doors to one of the most accessible supermarkets in the world, a supermarket that only caters to your dreams. So why not shop for the things you want, need, or desire for your own spiritual or financial growth, or happiness?

Once the correct energies are mixed together, then it is time to send them off to the universe for manifestation. This is done by using the art of positive visualization. The key to visualizing is to actually see what you want or desire in front of your mind's eye. Your visualization must be as clear as watching a television show. Once you've done this, then it is time to sit and wait patiently for what you've asked for, but you must always keep your desires in mind, see them, and believe in them.

The first rule of spellcasting is to always stay positive, no matter the odds or the conditioning of your mind. If you say something is going to work, it will work—and this attitude you should always have, not only with magic but with everything else you do in life.

THE TOOL STASH

There is no right or wrong way to start your spells on the go, and this is because they are simple and there are no lengthy rituals behind them. But there may be a time when a day of the week or a certain moon phase will be needed to enhance the spell.

To start off with, you may want to stock up on a few items and keep them all together for easy access, such as:

• Different-colored ribbons and cloths

You will be using them at times to enhance the needs you wish to manifest. Make sure the ribbons are all cotton.

• Candle holders

These do not have to be expensive, just durable.

• Colored candles

The candles need to be true to their color, which means that if they are blue on the outside, they will need to be blue on the inside as well. You don't want to confuse the universe when you are making your intentions known.

• Crystals

Try to obtain a small variety of crystals. The main ones you want to buy are amethyst and clear quartz.

• Essential oils and an oil burner

An oil burner is not only used for aromatherapy for medicinal purposes or to alleviate stress; it can also be used in magic. Essential oils are also often used in magical workings. An oil burner is usually ceramic, but the type of oil burner you choose is up to you. You may even have one already!

- Drawstring bags

    You can purchase or make drawstring bags. Making them is simple. Just cut a square piece of material, its color depending on the actual spell. Then make a little bag out of the material and keep it closed so that its contents don't fall out.

- Herbs

    You can find herbs just about anywhere. Try the supermarket first. Then, if you can't find a particular herb, go to a nursery or your friendly New Age store, where the employees will be able to help you. If you can only find fresh herbs, that's okay, but you need to dry them unless the spell specifies to use them fresh. To dry them, lay them flat in a shaded area on a piece of a brown paper bag for a few days until the leaves are crunchy to the touch.

- Censer and charcoal tablets

    You can use a small bowl for your censer or a tiny cauldron with three legs. It does not matter if it is metal or glass. You can just burn dry herbs on their own by lighting a match to the dry herbs, but if you want to get more out of your dry herbs or resins, just fill the bottom of the censer with either dirt or sand, even rock salt, to insulate the container, and then place a charcoal tablet on top. It's better to light it outside the house, since it initially gives off a not-so-pleasing gray smoke. Then, when it becomes red-hot, you can add your herbs on the top of the charcoal. Be aware that the charcoal tablets are a fire hazard and should be treated with care. Do not drop them on the floor or use them around small children—the burns are very painful.

These are just a few of the tools that you will need to conduct spells on the go. Once you get to know the spells and do them, it will be easy to replenish your tool stash so that you'll always have the things you need at your fingertips at a minute's notice.

23
DAYS OF THE WEEK AND PLANETS

We take the days of the week for granted. We mainly associate them with our daily schedules. We think about Monday, Tuesday, Wednesday, Thursday, and Friday as working days, chore days, and school days. Saturdays are the days we spend doing the things we didn't have time to do during the week, and Sunday is the day we basically catch up with family, friends, movies, or even the book we're reading.

The days of the week are closely associated with the planets, and our ancestors used them to capture the planets' essences into their magical and healing rituals. We can do the same because these are universal energies that have been around since the inception of all that we have ever known. Each planet has a close association to a day of the week.

You can use the days of the week with the planets to conduct spells. The planets and the days of the week are such powerful energies that they convey to the universe our needs and desires. For example, if you are doing a money spell, you may want to do it on a Thursday, which is the day for financial gain and wealth. Love spells are best conducted on Fridays, since Friday is associated with Venus, the goddess of love.

DAYS OF THE WEEK AND PLANETS ON THE GO
SUNDAY—SUN

The sun is the bright star at the center of our solar system. Its day is Sunday, and you can use this powerful energy, along with your creativity, in anything you wish to accomplish. Sunday is a great day to do a spell to sell your home or a business, or to buy a house or a car. This is also a great day to communicate with your spiritual guides. The sun gives hope when there is none to be found.

MONDAY—MOON

Monday is the day of our beloved moon, and this is a day when anything is possible. If you don't know what day to do a spell, do it on a Monday. The moon is filled with emotion and love. On this day we can conduct healing spells. You can also use this day to listen to your gut feelings and make serious decisions. You can use your psychic abilities to see into the future on a Monday.

TUESDAY—MARS

Tuesday is filled with confidence. This is due to the influence of Mars, which is very masculine and full of determination. We can use Tuesdays for protection, working against negative forces, and getting rid of bad spirits or anything else that is bad for us. Tuesday is also a day for getting things done or for finishing an overdue project.

WEDNESDAY—MERCURY

We all know Wednesday as "hump day," the middle of the working week. This is an excellent day to conduct business spells. Mercury helps with any type of family communication or in discussions with adversaries. Wednesdays are for winning arguments, or for making travel arrangements and wishing for a vacation. Mercury helps others say what they actually want or mean; if you want to know if someone loves you, this is the day to conduct spells for a truthful answer in order to help others see your point of view.

THURSDAY—JUPITER

Jupiter is the biggest planet in our solar system, and for this reason I use Thursdays for my money needs. You can use Thursdays to conduct wishing spells, luck spells, and abundance spells. Jupiter can be used for working on relationships or to find a happy medium during disagreements. You can also use Jupiter to conduct calming anger spells and addiction spells.

FRIDAY—VENUS

Friday is Venus, and she is the goddess of love. This is a time for love spells. On Fridays you can do attraction spells, friendship spells, work on your sexuality, and bring things out into the open. The best love spells are done on Fridays with a full moon. On this day, Venus gets ready to party and you should do the same. Venus and Friday bring pleasure to our world.

SATURDAY—SATURN

Saturday is a day for magical discipline. If you are true to your faith, this is the day to let the universe know. On Saturdays, you will be conducting protection spells and spells to get rid of negative energies. Saturday is the planning day. Saturn is very strict and stubborn, and this is why negative energy spells should be conducted on this day, because Saturn gives you the determination to stay focused. Saturday is a day to break free from a bad love affair or a person who doesn't take no for an answer. Hold Saturday close to your heart; for protection, Saturday is your day.

24
COLOR

The importance of color in our lives is well known. We need color, and without color our lives would be very bland indeed. Color is part of our everyday lives, and the colors of our clothes are at the top of the list. Every morning we decide what to put on. Some days we like a certain outfit, but on other days that same outfit may not appeal to us. This is because of the energy we unconsciously put out. We don't realize it, but our bodies scream for a certain color—and they let us know this by making that color attractive to our eyes.

Some colors, like red and orange, give out strong vibrations of warmth. Other colors, such as pink and light blue, give out passive vibrations that are soothing to the soul. Even many doctors have opted to swap their clinical white coats for blue ones, a move that has proven to lessen patients' fears and even their blood pressure.

Also, and most important, color enhances the needs we want to convey to the universe. Color is an essential part of magic and should always be consulted. Each color has a powerful meaning, and this meaning enhances our magical needs—not to mention our psychological and healing needs.

I use color on a daily basis. When I feel that I need protection, I wear black. When I feel down, I wear red to help lift myself up. When I need money, I strap a green cotton band around my wrist and shout to the universe that I'm in need. Green is the universal color for money, since it represents growth and prosperity. I'm immediately in tune with universal forces because of the green band around my wrist, which colors my entire etheric field like a green light bulb and acts as a beacon, sending my needs to the universe.

I've found that color bands are an easy way to make my magical needs known. They are also easy to create. Just cut some cotton material in the color of your needs and wrap this material around your right wrist (or around your left wrist if you are left-handed). Wrap this material around your wrist three times, and each time say your needs out loud to the universe, visualize them like a television commercial, and then make a knot to keep the band in place. Don't take the band, or bands, off until you feel your needs are being satisfied; make your color bands pleasing to the eye, as you may have to wear them for a few days.

COLOR BANDS ON THE GO

To find peace: Light-blue band

To heal illness: White band

For luck, money, and growth: Green band

To heal the heart: Dark-pink band

To enhance learning and studying: Yellow or orange band

For strength: Orange or red band

Love: Pink band

To combat negativity: Black or red band

To avoid stress: Blue band

Protection: Black band and a red band

To work against depression: Red band and an orange band

Fertility: Orange—but wrap it around your waist only one time

To fight sadness: Blue and pink bands wrapped together

Attraction: Red—but don't tie a knot, just a simple bow

Soul connection: Lavender band

Psychic workings: Purple bands around both wrists

To deal with anger: Light-blue band

Communication with angels: Gold band

To listen to your gut feelings: Yellow band

Women's health issues: Orange band

Before exams: Bright yellow band

Astral travel: Purple band and a white band

To calm down a very active toddler: Light-blue band

For a job interview: Orange band and a blue band together, but don't wear them—just stick them in your pants or jacket pocket.

To enhance the chakras: Get red, orange, yellow, green, blue, purple, and pink ribbons and make a plait out of them all. Once you've done this, wrap it around your wrist like a bracelet, and your chakras will always be in tune to your needs.

Protection for babies: For both girl and boy babies, tie a red ribbon to a safety pin and fasten it to the baby's clothes where no one can see it.

OVERALL MAGICAL COLORS

White: Healing

Yellow: Psychic abilities

Red: Courage and strength

Purple: Communication and peace

Blue: Protection and calm

Pink: Love and relationships

Black: Protection against negative forces

Green: Healing, money, and spiritual growth

25
CRYSTALS

Crystals are precious and extremely beautiful. They have aided our ancestors spiritually and physically for millennia. Once you tap into a crystal's unique beauty and strength, the effect is transformational. When worn or carried, crystals transmit a feeling of peace. Like a candle in the mist of darkness, a sense of spiritual enlightenment warms the heart. Anger becomes a thing of the past, and you exude love and compassion to those around you.

Today, the legacy of crystals is stronger than ever before. Crystals are a wonderful complementary tool in magic. The energies within each individual crystal work in unison with each individual. When the energy of a crystal merges with your own, sparks take to the air and those sparks take your wishes and needs to the universe.

Crystals absorb as well as project energy, which means that lots of other people may have handled your crystal and imbued it with their own energy before you did. For that reason, it's important to cleanse your crystal before you program it with your intent. There are many ways to cleanse a crystal, with no right or wrong way to do so—I will guide you through this process. If a spell in this section does not indicate a cleansing method, you still need to cleanse your crystal, which you can do by placing it in a glass of water and adding a large spoonful of salt. Mix the salt with the water and crystal, and leave the mixture outside for one night in your backyard or on a balcony before doing the spell.

The effects of crystals are wide and varied, but in general they are potent protective and healing talismans that can transform your life in any way you want them to, providing you have the desire to change, the will to believe, and you forever hold the love and understanding the crystals will bring.

CRYSTALS ON THE GO

ACCIDENTS

A carnelian agate is best. Just rinse this crystal with some rainwater, hold it in your hands, and visualize prevention where you need it the most. Keep the crystal with you at all times.

AGGRESSION

For those who share their unwanted aggression with you, keep a bloodstone crystal close to your heart at all times and the aggressor will no longer be aggressive.

ALCOHOLISM

If you want to stop drinking, cleanse an amethyst crystal deep within the earth for an entire day. Then keep this very powerful crystal with you at all times. Every day, visualize that you dislike drinking alcohol until you actually do, and your addiction will diminish.

ANGELS

When you seek the guidance of an angel, hold a clear quartz crystal close to your heart and ask for divine direction and you shall find it.

ANGER

When you want to calm someone's unnecessary anger, leave a blue-lace agate crystal out on the grass on a full-moon night. The next morning, hold this crystal in your hands and visualize this person's anger subsiding and as a thing of the past. Then hide the crystal where it will never be found by the one who needs calming down.

ANXIETY

The jitters of anxiety can be quieted down by wearing a pyrite crystal. Cleanse this crystal with a drop of lavender essential oil, and as you do so, visualize that which gives you anxiety. Hang this crystal from your neck, and every time you are anxious, touch the crystal with your index finger. Feel the calming, soothing sensations that only pyrite can give running through your body.

ASTHMA

Always wear a rose quartz crystal for your asthma, or have one under your pillow.

AURA

To strengthen your aura, hold a clear quartz crystal and it will magnify your aura tenfold.

BAD TEMPER

For those who would rather fight than talk, place amethyst and blue agate crystals under their pillows.

BROKEN HEART

To heal a broken heart, place a rose quartz crystal on top of a grassy patch and leave it out all night. Carry this crystal close to your heart at all times, and it will heal the pain you are suffering deep down inside.

CANCER

For those who suffer from cancer, a smoky quartz and an amethyst crystal should always be worn. The quartz heals while the amethyst pacifies. This will aid and strengthen your faith while treatment is being conducted and remission is at hand.

CHILDREN

The best crystal for children to have is a tiger's-eye. Cleanse it with baby oil and hold it in your hands, while visualizing the protection and growth you wish for your children. Then place this crystal in the children's room, where it cannot be found by them.

CLARITY OF MIND

When the mind is boggled with problems, hold an aquamarine crystal in your hands, and as you do so, visualize your mind clear, with your problems solved and with no more worries.

CLAIRVOYANCE

To aid spiritual workings, have in front of you a lapiz lazuli or a ruby crystal. These two crystals take the mind further than any other.

CONFIDENCE / COURAGE

If it's confidence you need, then it's confidence you shall have. Cleanse an onyx crystal under the sun for an hour. Then, while it is still hot in your hands, visualize the confidence you need and you will have it.

CREATIVE EXPRESSION

If you need creativity, carry with you a bloodstone crystal.

DANGER

If you feel danger is ahead, carry with you a malachite crystal.

DEPRESSION

Depression can bring you down, but a kunzite crystal will help to lift you up.

DREAMS

For total dream recall, cleanse an azurite crystal with lavender water and always have it under your pillow. Think of your dreams before you get out of bed, as that way they will stay longer in your mind for you to analyze them.

ENERGY

If it's energy you're lacking, wear as much silver jewelry as you can. Silver is a conductor of energy, and it will give you plenty.

ENEMIES/ENVY

For the enemies and envy in your office, put a tiger's-eye crystal on your desk. It will repel those enemies you don't need to have, and the envious ones will go away.

EVIL EYE

I know of only one crystal that can protect you from the evil eye, and that is tiger's-eye when it is worn.

FAITHFULNESS

For a faithful partner, place a blue agate crystal under your partner's pillow.

FERTILITY / PREGNANCY

To become pregnant, carry a tiger's-eye, carnelian agate, and a red jasper crystal with you at all times. To have a healthy pregnancy, carry a howlite crystal inside your bra.

FINANCIAL STABILITY / FORTUNE

To keep that financial stability going, wear opals or carry a bloodstone crystal in your purse or wallet.

FRIENDS

To keep and make friends, a bloodstone crystal should do the trick.

HAPPINESS

Keep together a moonstone and a moss agate crystal in a little orange drawstring bag, and it will make you happy with every beat of your heart.

HEADACHES / MIGRAINES

Stress headaches can be avoided if you cleanse a hematite crystal and wear it as a necklace.

HOPE

When you think hope has gone, find a citrine crystal and keep it in your pocket, but not before you cleanse it with a drop of bergamot, which is the "happy" essential oil.

INTELLECT / INTUITION

A rhodochrosite crystal that has been cleansed in rainwater and worn around the neck will boost the intuition and intellect.

JEALOUSY

Without a jealous partner knowing, place under his or her pillow an apophyllite crystal, and there will be nothing for your partner to feel jealous about.

LOVE

For self-love, the best crystal to have is a rose quartz.

LOVER

A tiger's-eye crystal exchanged between lovers will aid with the future of what is yet to come.

LUCK

There is no such thing as bad luck when you carry a tiger's-eye crystal.

MEDITATION

When meditating, it is always good to hold a crystal in your hand; that crystal should always be a clear quartz or an amethyst crystal.

MEMORY

Some days you may not remember the color of your under-wear, so carry a fluorite crystal—and you'll remember not just the color of your underwear but also the brand name.

MENOPAUSE

If you think you are near the crone years, carry with you a ruby crystal and keep it close to your heart.

MONEY

Over the years, I have discovered that the money-attracting crystals are citrine and red jasper. The citrine brings abundance, and the red jasper attracts new work opportunities that bring in the cash.

NEGATIVE ENERGIES

To combat the negative energies of unwanted entities, cleanse a tiger's-eye and an apache-tear crystal in a glass of water with a teaspoon of rock salt. Leave this mixture outside on a full-moon night, and on the third day bring it inside. Now hold the crystals in your hands and visualize the negative energy you want to ward away. Carry the crystals with you every day.

317

PEACE

We all want a peaceful home, free of arguments. A rose crystal and an amethyst quartz crystal will do the job. To keep the energy flowing, keep the crystals where your family congregates.

PROTECTION

For the protection of the self, always carry a tiger's-eye crystal.

PSYCHIC ABILITIES

To magnify your psychic abilities, always have with you a lapis lazuli crystal.

SADNESS

When there is sadness in your heart due to a breakup or because you've lost a loved one, hold or carry an amethyst crystal in your hand, and the pain will lessen every day.

SLEEP

If you're unable to sleep, keep an amethyst crystal in a sock under your pillow, and add to it a drop of lavender essential oil. You will then be able to sleep all night without looking at the clock.

STRENGTH

If you need the personal strength to face situations that seem uneven, drop an aquamarine crystal in a glass. Keep it out where the moonlight shines at night, and in the morning drink the water—but please don't swallow the crystal!

STRESS

To fight stress, the best remedy is to hang a moonstone crystal around your neck 24/7. The stress will go away, but if it ever returns, again hang a moonstone crystal around your neck at all times.

VERBAL EXPRESSION

The best crystal to hold in your hand when you need to express yourself is an aquamarine crystal; it will never let you down when you need to make a point.

VIOLENCE

If you ever suffer from violent abuse, carry with you a bloodstone crystal, and you will seek the help you need to be able to walk away.

MAGICAL CRYSTALS FOR THE HOME

Clear quartz protects your home and your loved ones from unwanted negative energies.

Amethyst is calming and soothing. It brings peaceful and calming energies to the home. It helps those who have a little bit of a temper, and it brings relief to those who suffer from stress.

Citrine can bring abundance to the home, whether it be an abundance of love, happiness, and/or money. When worn, it can also help the young ones to retain the information they learn in school. Citrine also helps its wearers find the patience they need to confront uncomfortable situations.

Agates come in all colors and can bring out the courage necessary to stand up for yourself. Pink agate is for love; green agate is for money; brown agate is good for those who are trying to quit an addiction to something, such as cigarettes or alcohol; and blue agate is for healing. Agate is one of those crystals that you should always have in your home.

Rose quartz can help us find love, but it can also help us love ourselves above all—because if we don't love who we are, then no one else will. Like amethyst, rose quartz can calm the beast in all of us if we place it under the pillow before bedtime.

Remember that crystals are a gift from nature. It is said that if everyone in the world wears or has a crystal in the home, the earth will regenerate from all we have taken away from her. If you are asking yourself, "Is this true?" —well, I certainly don't doubt it!

CRYSTALS FOR EACH DAY OF THE WEEK

Sunday: To heal the self and learn something new, use a citrine crystal

Monday: To find purity and protection in your life, use a clear quartz crystal

Tuesday: For strength and passion all the way, use a garnet crystal

Wednesday: To find wisdom and togetherness without the stress, use an amethyst crystal

Thursday: To find patience and tranquillity, use a sodalite crystal

Friday: For the growth of love in your life, use an aventurine crystal

Saturday: To rid all the week's negativity and to stay positive for the week ahead, use an onyx crystal

26
ALL THAT GROWS

Everything on this earth vibrates with beautiful, uninhibited forces. These innocent but strong, willful energies are found anywhere. Anything that is green and growing is filled with a strong sense of wisdom and strength. This wisdom and strength can be utilized to grow and prosper on a spiritual level. These energies can be anything from the bark of a tree to the grass under your feet; just because they can't talk, it doesn't mean they are dead or unworthy. On the contrary, they are very much alive, and believe it or not, they are waiting for us to seek their aid.

Some laugh at those who talk to plants as though they were people. But it has been proven that this interaction with plants has positive results, and more people are doing it; some people even sing and play music to plants.

I sometimes get a few stares when I hug a tree on my daily walks with nature, but I can't help it—hugging trees makes me feel good. From strong, healthy trees I seek energy and wisdom, and for the ones that look a bit sad, I pass on healing energies through my touch. This is a wonderful experience. I'm not only out with nature, but I certainly feel a part of it.

Everything that is green falls into this wonderful category: plants, trees, herbs, and even flowers have a special purpose for their existence. Our ancestors knew this truth and they have passed it down to us—not just for medicinal needs but for magical needs as well. For example, not only did they use chamomile for colic, fevers, indigestion, and as a hair rinse to bring the natural highlights out, but they also used chamomile's magical powers in love baths and in protection and purifying sachets.

I always have fresh basil and rosemary in my house. I make arrangements out of these herbs soon after I pick them from my garden. Rosemary is good for cooking as well as protection, and basil keeps the finances healthy and protected! These strong, powerful herbs can do no wrong, but you don't need to blend them together; each one has its own special qualities and works rather well on its own to bring a much needed effect or change. I just like putting them together, and their scent really purifies my home.

In magic, all that is green is used to its fullest. We crush, burn, and dry everything for a purpose. We crush to blend, we burn to purify, and we can even dry all that is green to place in little drawstring bags for a specific purpose.

We are going to use these wonderful energies, and use them to their highest potential to enhance the needs and wants we hope to achieve. Let's do the quick fixes by visualizing our needs, and making them happen by using a little bit of this and a little bit of that!

HERBS FOR PROTECTION ON THE GO
PROTECT YOUR HOME FROM UNWANTED ENTITIES

Sprinkle angelica all over the house on Saturday before sundown, and unwanted entities will no longer want to visit.

KEEP THIEVES AWAY

To ward away thieves, hang from your back door a little red drawstring bag and fill it up with caraway seeds. But be sensible: always lock your front door and back door when you're not home.

VACATIONS

To stay safe while you're on vacation, take a cotton ball and soak it in witch hazel oil. Rub the cotton ball filled with the oil inside the shoes you will be wearing most often on your trip. Leave your shoes out on a full-moon night and seek protection from the moon and its light.

It's best to do this on a Saturday, and protected you will be during your vacation.

PROTECT YOUR HOME
FROM OUTSIDE NEGATIVE FORCES

When you are ready to mop your floors, add to the bucket a teaspoon of cumin powder and a tablespoon of rock salt; as you mop, visualize the protection you seek for your home.

PROTECTION AGAINST GOSSIP

In a little black drawstring bag, place a small handful of un-cooked rice and a bunch of fresh rosemary leaves. Hold this little bag in your hand and visualize the gossip not getting near you. See it fading away like smoke.

UNINVITED GUESTS

Behind your front door, always have a large head of garlic. Anyone who wants to come in without an invitation will think twice before crossing the threshold.

PROTECTION FOR YOUR CHILDREN

Under your children's pillows, place a laurel leaf and visualize the protection you feel they need. Or get some fennel, crush it in a mortar and pestle, and sprinkle it in their shoes. Protected they will be without even knowing it.

FRESH PROTECTION

Make a bunch of herbal arrangements every Saturday. In a vase full of water, add rosemary, basil, parsley, and mint. Within this arrangement, place a few leaves from a fern to make it look good. Keep this arrangement on the center table of your living room. Protected you will be, and don't forget to refresh the arrangement every week.

HERBS FOR LOVE ON THE GO
TO ATTRACT THE LOVE YOU WANT

Eat an apple and pick out the seeds. Place the seeds on a white cloth and let them dry in a shaded area until they desiccate. Sprinkle lavender talcum powder on them and keep them under your pillow to attract the love you've always wanted.

TO BE LOVED

Take all the petals from a dry red rose and a dry white rose and mix the petals together. Add a dash of cinnamon and a star anise. Mix this all together and place it in a small pink box with a handwritten note that says you will be loved forevermore. Sign your name to the note and close the box.

FOR ATTRACTION

Carry with you three vanilla beans! And attractive to others you will be.

TO HEAL A BROKEN HEART

Find an elm tree and wrap your arms around it. Wish it to heal your broken heart, and leave behind a coin on the ground as a healing payment.

TO SPICE UP THE MARRIAGE BED

Crush patchouli and dill together. Two hours before bed, sprinkle this powder on the sheets. Wait and see, and the fun you seek will be.

FOR A NIGHT ON THE TOWN

Before you go out on the town, sprinkle cinnamon inside your shoes. They will take you where the fun is and to the people you want to meet.

TO FIND LOVE

Always have with you a myrtle leaf inside your bosom.

TO KEEP LOVE

To keep the love you have, tie together two sandalwood sticks with a red ribbon and place them under the middle of your mattress.

TO FIND OUT IF SOMEONE
IS IN LOVE WITH YOU

Write the full name of the person on a piece of paper. Cover the paper with a whole bunch of chestnuts, and that person will tell you yes or no.

TO SEND A LOVE LETTER

After you have written your love letter, sprinkle lavender leaves on it and let the leaves sit on top of the paper for a day or so. Make sure your mind has nothing but loving thoughts for the person for whom the letter was intended. Take the piece of paper outside and blow the lavender in the direction of the wind; then fold the letter, mail it, and you will see.

HERBS FOR LUCK AND MONEY
ON THE GO
FOR A LUCKY HOME

Have lots of violet plants in your home.

TO HAVE MONEY
IN YOUR PURSE OR WALLET

Sprinkle nutmeg between the bills and it will just multiply them evenly.

FOR WEALTH

Have a bowl of pecans by the front door but don't eat them; if you do eat them, you will be eating your financial needs.

FOR LUCK

Carry with you a lucky hand root, and lucky you will be in all you do.

TO MAKE A BUSINESS FRUITFUL

Behind your business door always have a bowl of sesame seeds, and on top of them sprinkle a little bit of gold-dust powder.

TO HAVE SUCCESS IN LIFE

For success, carry with you a piece of a ginger root and replace it with a new one every month and a day.

MONEY PILLOW

Make a little pillow with green cotton material and fill it up with Irish moss. Carry it with you at all times for your money needs.

TO WIN THE LOTTERY

Put it out there that you want to win the lottery jackpot. Mix together ginger, nutmeg, and sage. Sprinkle the mixture on top of your lottery ticket and put your ticket high up, in a safe place, until the night of the drawing. Do this every time you dream about winning!

NUTS WE ARE!

Always have out a bowl filled with mixed nuts. Every morning before you leave the house, take a nut with you for luck and, at the end of the day, leave it at the front door of your bank.

COIN JAR

Keep a jar filled with coins and add to it saffron powder from the supermarket. The jar will keep multiplying the coins.

PINECONES

Hang from your key ring a small pinecone, and every morning dip it in rosemary leaves for your money and luck needs.

27
INCENSE

When I was young, and even to this day, my mother smoked out her house with rosemary leaves. She would take three or four barbecue charcoals and place them on the stove, waiting until each charcoal was blood-red. Then she picked up the charcoals with a pair of kitchen tongs, placed them in a silver baking dish, and added a handful of rosemary leaves. She took this very powerful, blinding smoke all around the house. Well, she used to do so before my sister and I introduced her to the charcoal tablet, a much easier and safer way to purify the house, but some habits are hard to break. She still likes the old way better, and when she doesn't have any charcoal tablets, she goes back to her old ways quite happily.

There is the type of incense that is store-bought, and then there are the types of incense you make yourself. I can honestly say that I use both kinds. I use store-bought incense for its fragrance; for a particular scent on its own—like rose, lavender, or patchouli—I just light it up with the thought in mind of what my needs are, and the incense works rather well along with positive visualization.

Now, the make-it-yourself type of incense is always the best. I believe the more smoke you make, the more energy you put out (maybe this is an inherited trait!), but please don't trigger the smoke detectors like I've done in the past!

Incense smoke is one of the quickest ways to let the universe know your needs, and that's why I use it for quick fixes in spells on the go. The air element holds your wish in a bubble of smoke and directs it where you want it to go. You only need the actual dry herb (unless otherwise specified), the charcoal tablet in a censer, and your needs. You can burn herbs or coarse resins like frankincense tear drops, myrrh, or dragon's blood, which are very powerful when working with negative forces.

For the perfect outcome, combine these energies with the days of the week in order to bring, luck, riches, peace, harmony, and love—not to mention the purification effects they produce when you are using them for healing, psychic work, or even to get rid of a negative entity or energy. So, the next time you see an incense stick, remember that it is much more than just an aromatic fragrance!

SMOKE ON THE GO
HOUSE CLEANSING: ROSEMARY

Close all your doors and windows, but leave the front door open. Take this smoke throughout the house, going from the back to the front door. As soon as you finish, you will feel sparkling and new refreshing energies.

SELF-CLEANSING: FRANKINCENSE TEARS

Place your charcoal tablet in its censer with two frankincense tears and then place it on the floor. Stand naked in front of it and let the smoke engulf your body. Feel all the negativity inside of you leaving your body, to be replaced by only good energies.

PROTECTION: DRAGON'S BLOOD

Burn dragon's blood in your censer once a week for the protection of your home.

PEACE: LAVENDER

Lavender leaves on a charcoal tablet will keep your home peaceful, as well as all of those within its walls.

NEGATIVE ENERGIES: RUE

If you can tolerate the smell of dry rue on top of a hot charcoal tablet, you can tolerate anything—but negative energies hate it, which is why I use it.

LOVE: ROSE PETALS

Unfortunately, the scent of burning dry rose petals is not as pleasant as you would think, but if you mix them in a mortar and pestle with rosemary leaves, you will have a very tolerable and powerful love smoke that you may want to take to the bathroom with you while you have a bath. As you bathe, think only of the love you wish to have in your life.

CREATING GOOD ENERGIES: MYRRH

Myrrh is quite pleasant to the nose. Take your censer all around your home in a counterclockwise motion, and as you do, you will create good energies.

REMOVING AN UNWANTED ENTITY: THISTLE

Burn this herb in the area where you believe the entity is and yell out to it three times as the thistle burns: "Get out, get out, get out of my home and life!"

HEALING: SANDALWOOD AND FRANKINCENSE

Sprinkle sandalwood on top of your charcoal tablet, and then add one tear of frankincense. Meditate on the healing you wish and visualize the smoke going toward the one in need.

MONEY: BASIL AND PARSLEY

Crush together dry parsley and basil and then burn the mixture once a week, using the days of the week and planets; your money needs will be answered.

GOOD LUCK:
NUTMEG AND CINNAMON

From your spice rack at home, mix together half a teaspoon of nutmeg and cinnamon. The combination may smell like the festive season, but the luck it brings will always be in season!

HEX BREAKING:
ANGELICA AND CLOVES

Visualize the hex you would like to break. Then place three cooking cloves and a dash of angelica on top of the charcoal. See the hex breaking like a piece of glass on a tile floor. Repeat every day for three days.

28
THE SCENTS
OF OILS

The magic of oils was part of our ancestors' lives, and we can honor them by incorporating oils into our quick magical fixes. I've always had good results with essential oils. I keep all my little bottles of oils in a cedar box, which absorbs each and every single one of their mystical and magical scents. When I take out this box, my entire house is bewitched by the energies of the oils and their powerful fragrances, which automatically lets me know that I'm ready to start my magical workings.

Essential oils are derived from aromatic plants, which are processed to produce a particular oil. This oil is as pure as it gets and vibrates with earthbound energies. These aromatic oils are alive and filled with magical properties even after the distillation process.

People are becoming more aware of the healing and relaxing properties of oils by way of aromatherapy and invigorating massages that leave them feeling totally relaxed and re-energized. Just as you need real essential oils for these types of therapies, you also need the real deal when using essential oils for magic. Synthetics just don't cut it!

Each one of these oils has its own properties, just as herbs do. These oils are so powerful that, with just a single drop, you can send your magical needs to the universe loud and clear. But be careful: some people are allergic to oils because of the strength they possess. I've known people to be allergic to the scent of pure lavender oil. These folks get sick to their stomachs because lavender oil can be so sickly sweet. A single drop can linger for hours in an oil burner. So take care when using these oils, and mind their powerful scents and the possible reactions they can produce.

The best and quickest way to get results from your oil burner is to place the oils on the burner first, and then light the candle and add hot—not cold!—water. As soon as the hot water makes contact with the oils, you will have an immediate magical connection with the universe.

You can purchase essential oils just about anywhere now; massage therapists, spas, and even supermarkets sell lavender and tea-tree oils. If you're in doubt, the price tag will alert you to an oil's authenticity. Real essential oils aren't cheap, and the bottle is so little that it seems ridiculous to pay so much money for what can seem like a large tablespoon—but don't forget you're getting pure essential oils for your magical needs.

ESSENTIAL OILS ON THE GO
RELAXATION
Put three drops of lavender oil in your oil burner.

FINDING SLEEP
Put one drop of jasmine and two drops of clary sage in your oil burner half an hour before bedtime, or sprinkle one drop of clary sage on your pillow one hour before bedtime.

MONEY
Burn three drops of basil oil in your oil burner for your money needs whenever possible!

HAPPINESS IN THE HOME

In your oil burner, place two drops of bergamot and one of neroli for a happy home environment.

CONCENTRATION AT WORK

Place two drops of rosemary oil in your handkerchief and smell it every time you feel you need concentration or are about to fall asleep from a lack of motivation.

HOMEWORK ALERTNESS

Place two drops of peppermint oil and two drops of thyme in your oil burner for alertness and to help your kids concentrate.

MEDITATION

Place one drop of chamomile oil on your index finger and massage the tips of both of your index fingers together before meditation. Gently rub this oil on your temples.

ATTRACTION

Do I need to say it? Wear rose oil whenever possible!

PROTECTION

Burn in your oil burner two drops of frankincense and one drop of myrrh oil.

If you need a quick protection fix, get an old pot you don't use anymore and fill it up with one liter of water. Bring the water to a boil. Now, take the pot away from the heat and add one crushed garlic clove, two drops of black pepper oil, two drops of frankincense oil, and three drops of rosemary oil. Then take this steaming protection smoke all over the house. Repeat three times, and each time bring the pot back to a boil.

PEACE

Always burn lavender oil in your home and at work, in order to drive away disturbances and agitation. Or burn two drops of marjoram to keep the peace.

MAGIC

Before any magical workings, burn nutmeg oil in your oil burner. Just one drop will do the job.

APHRODISIAC

To enhance sexual drive, burn in your oil burner one drop of vanilla and two drops of patchouli oil.

KEEPING YOUR MAN

Apply one drop of marjoram on his clothes and he will always be yours.

HEALING

After an illness, burn sandalwood in your home. Two drops will be enough to bring health back into your world.

HAPPY ESSENTIAL OILS

Bergamot, grapefruit, orange, clary sage, and basil.

DE-STRESS ESSENTIAL OILS

Lavender, chamomile, and ylang-ylang.

PROTECTION ESSENTIAL OILS

Basil, myrrh, frankincense, rosemary, and garlic.

29
THE LIGHT OF
A CANDLE'S FLAME

I just can't see magic without the flame of a candle! Magic and light go hand in hand, and the flame of a candle is certainly linked to the human spirit. The flame of a candle emits universal energies, and not only do candles bring light for us to be able to see, but they are also a way for us to communicate with the heavens.

The flame of a candle is very powerful. The flame conveys our needs and wants to the universe with strength and sincerity. Candles are my forte. I like to light them when I'm at home—I feel better when I do. Candles keep me focused on a particular intent. Sometimes I have about five candles going all over the house at the same time, and each one is lit for a specific purpose.

My daughter was taking one of her high school exams, and regrettably I wasn't going to be home. I quickly called my mother to ask her to light a yellow candle while visualizing my daughter answering all the questions with confidence and knowledge. My mother was more than willing to do this, knowing that her granddaughter would benefit from a quick fix that only takes a few minutes to do—that is, if you have the right color candle on hand as she did. You can see now why it's so important to keep that "tool stash" fully supplied.

The color of the candles plays a great part in any candle-burning ritual, and just by simply lighting a candle of a certain color you are causing an effect. Each color, as described in chapter 24, has a specific meaning, but instead of *wearing* a specific color, now you're going to use a candle's flame to send your needs to the universe.

I like to dress my candles, no matter if I'm doing a ritual or a quick fix. It doesn't take me long to dress a candle, and if I'm in a hurry, I just take the olive oil bottle from my pantry and splash a little bit on my hand. I then rub my hands together and anoint the candle. My right hand anoints the top of the candle where the wick is, and my left hand does the bottom of the candle. Dressing the candle is just another step in making your needs known to the universe. While you anoint the candle, you're already thinking about your reasons for lighting the candle in the first place, and in turn you are making the universe aware that you're in need.

Once you've finished dressing the candle, light it and then stand in front of it and visualize your needs. Make sure your visualization is clear, without any doubts or negative thoughts. Let your mind take your needs to the universe with sincerity, trust, and love, and trust me—you'll never look back. Magic and light go hand in hand, and both are linked to the human spirit. A candle's flame is mysterious in many ways—as well as beautiful to watch when you are seeking solitude and peace of heart.

CANDLES ON THE GO
ANGER WITHIN

For any type of anger, light a light-blue candle in the name of the person who is angry with the world.

BEFORE COURT DAY

It's no fun going to court, so light a purple candle and a green candle on a Thursday for good results.

BEFORE MEDITATION

Light a purple candle before any meditation or spiritual workings.

CONNECTION WITH YOUR SPIRITUAL GUIDE

Light a white candle and a purple candle to connect with your spiritual guide.

CONCENTRATION AND LEARNING

Light yellow candles when your children are doing homework or studying.

COURAGE FOR ALL YOUR NEEDS

Light a red candle and an orange candle on a Tuesday to find the courage you need.

EASING DEPRESSION

When depression sets in, light a white candle and a pink candle and your depression will diminish.

EGO BE GONE

If someone has an ego problem, light a green candle and a black candle in that person's name, and his or her ego will subside.

ENERGY AND STRENGTH

When you feel you need that get-up-and-go, light a red candle for yourself and you will see.

ENHANCE A GATHERING

When you have guests over, light a white candle and a pink candle and a great gathering you will have.

EVERYDAY PEACE

We all want peace in our homes, and it's always good to have white candles and blue candles burning at all times.

EVIL SPIRITS

When there are evil spirits around, light a black candle first and wish them gone. Then light a white candle, and wish the spirits a home that is not yours and is preferably in the heavens above.

FAITHFUL PARTNER

To keep your partner good in all aspects of your relationship, light a green candle and a blue candle on Wednesdays.

FINDING A JOB

Light a green candle and ask the universe to find you the right employment.

FINDING LOVE

When you are ready to find the love of your life, light a pink candle and a green candle on Fridays for someone to come along for you to love.

GAINING FAITH IN YOURSELF

When you feel your faith is gone, light a red candle and a white candle to find again the purpose of your soul.

GETTING IN TOUCH WITH YOUR ANGELS

To have angels around you, light white candles and purple candles.

GETTING RID OF HATE

When you hate, you block out every single ounce of good energy in your life, so light a black candle and a white candle and wish the hatred that is in your heart gone in order to bring good things back into your life.

HAPPINESS IN YOUR LIFE

Always light blue candles for the happiness you need.

HARMONY IS NEEDED

If it's harmony you need, a blue candle lit first thing in the morning will bring it to you.

HEALING FRIENDSHIPS

To heal a friendship or to make friends, light a white candle and a blue candle on Wednesdays.

HEALING FROM AN ILLNESS

To heal from an illness, light a white candle and a blue candle to get you back on track.

HEALTH AND WELL-BEING

For your health needs, light a white candle and a blue candle. You can also light them in the name of a loved one who needs healing.

IN THE MOOD FOR LOVE

Light a red candle in your bedroom just before bedtime to get you in the mood and ready for an amorous evening.

LOVE

Light a pink candle and a white candle when you feel you're lacking love in your life.

LUCK AT EVERY TURN

Always have yellow candles at home and light them for good luck.

MONEY—WE ALL WANT IT AND NEED IT

Light green candles whenever possible and send your money needs to the universe as many times as you feel you should.

MOVING ON AFTER AN EMOTIONAL BREAKUP

After the breakup of a relationship, light a blue candle and a yellow candle. Doing so will enable you to move on, or light the candles in the name of another who needs to move on.

PASSIONATE EVENING

If passion is needed, light a pink candle and a red candle.

PREGNANCY WISH

If you are dreaming of becoming a mother, light a yellow candle and a pink candle as much as you like when your timing is right.

PROTECTION AGAINST DANGER

When you feel danger is upon you, light a black candle and a blue candle to ward the danger away from you and the ones you love.

SEEKING A PROMOTION

We all want to be promoted, and you will have a better chance if you light a blue candle and a white candle on Thursdays.

SELLING YOUR HOME

Light a green candle every Sunday until your home is sold.

STOP NEGATIVITY IN THE HOME

To get rid of negativity in your home, light a black candle and a white candle every Saturday just before dawn.

SUCCESSFUL BUSINESS

Light a green candle and an orange candle behind your own business door.

WANTING TO BE UNDERSTOOD

Light an orange candle and a yellow candle when you need the understanding of others.

WHEN HELP IS NEEDED

This is one of my favorites. Light a red candle for your partner to help you around the house.

WHEN IN NEED OF PROTECTION

Light a black candle and a white candle when you feel that protection is required.

WORK ENVIRONMENT

To keep your work environment healthy, light a blue candle and a green candle at your place of employment.

YOUR DREAM HOME

Visualizing that you will one day have your own home is great, but lighting a blue candle and a pink candle will reinforce your dreams tenfold. Don't visualize "one day"; instead, visualize owning your home *today*.

CANDLES FOR EACH DAY OF THE WEEK

Sunday: Yellow, to aid the healing of the self and to learn something new that day

Monday: White, for purity and protection in your life

Tuesday: Red, for strength and passion all the way

Wednesday: Purple, for wisdom and family communication

Thursday: Blue, for patience and tranquillity during the day

Friday: Green, for growth and love in your life

Saturday: Black, to rid yourself of all the week's negativity and to stay positive for the week ahead

30
WATER AND
ITS ELEMENT

The first thing my mother used to tell me to do when I felt sick was to take a shower. "It'll make you feel better," she'd say. Today I tell my own daughter the same thing. Having a shower or a bath has always made me feel 100 percent better, especially when I sense negativity around me. I just get under the shower and wash it all off, and this method always works—with enduring positive results.

Water is associated with the emotions, and emotions are our greatest enemy. If our emotions are out of whack, our physical body will be out of whack as well. Unfortunately, when that happens we can't function and we can't possibly think rationally. The decisions we make in this state are governed solely by our emotional state of mind, and they are often decisions we end up wishing we hadn't made.

The water element is miraculous in its own way. I have always visualized water as a rough sponge and the negativity in our bodies as dirt. Once water touches the body, it becomes more like a tool to scrub away negative energy than anything else—and our positive visualizations become the soap or detergent. The more you visualize, the more cleansing suds you make and the better your chances of getting rid of what's bothering you, whether it be negativity from others or even from yourself.

Now, a bath is an excellent way to utilize the water element. Taking a bath is one of the most relaxing things anyone can do. Moreover, a bath oozes with positive, replenishing energies— energies that your body requires to replace what was taken away throughout the day.

Unfortunately, a bath by itself isn't one of the quick fixes, but using the element of water whenever possible is absolutely essential. If you don't have time for a bath, then try the bucket spells on the go. Okay, don't laugh—the bucket works! These spells are great for those of you who don't have a bathtub in your home or the time to relax in the tub.

Just get yourself a white bucket for your magical water connection with the universe. Once you've added to the bucket what is required by the spell, take the bucket with you and leave it outside the shower with the contents of the spell already in it. Take your shower as you would normally and when you finish, bring the bucket into the shower, fill it up with lukewarm water, and turn off the faucet. Then stand there naked, visualizing your needs to the universe. Place your hand inside the bucket and gently mix the ingredients while visualizing your needs. Once you've finished establishing your needs, hold the bucket up high and pour it over your head, gently letting the water run all over your body.

Once the bucket is empty, don't rinse yourself off. Just step out of the shower and pat yourself dry with a white towel. By doing this, you are sealing yourself and ensuring the bad energy you just got rid of doesn't come back. You're also making sure that the new energy you just put in stays in.

BUCKET SPELLS ON THE GO
WASH AWAY STRESS

In your bucket, place three drops of lavender oil and half a cup of chamomile flowers—and your stress will be a thing of the past.

WASH AWAY NEGATIVITY

Place in the bucket one teaspoon of cumin powder, a few leaves of fresh basil, and one teaspoon of rock salt. The negativity you hold will be gone.

TO ATTRACT MONEY

Crush three cooking cloves together with a large cinnamon stick and sesame seeds. Once you've done that, place the mixture in your white bucket. You can do this as many times as you want, and it is best to do it on Thursdays.

AFTER AN ALTERCATION

Any type of disagreement or fight can leave us in a state of mental and emotional discomfort. To wash away these uncomfortable feelings, place in your white bucket a large table-spoon of salt together with a teaspoon of olive oil.

TO ATTRACT LOVE

To attract the love you need and want, place in your bucket the petals of a red rose, two drops of spearmint oil, and a bunch of fresh basil.

TO STOP NASTY GOSSIP ABOUT YOU

Fill your bucket with warm-to-hot water. Add in one large tablespoon of sage, one large tablespoon of rosemary, and a bunch of parsley. Let it all sit for about thirty minutes; just before your shower, mix it all together. Once you've finished your shower and the bucket spell, pick up the parsley from the floor of your shower and place it in your garbage can with the gossip.

BEFORE BED

To have a good sleep, place in your bucket three drops of lav-ender oil and sleep you will find.

FOR A PASSIONATE EVENING

Place in your bucket all the petals of a fresh red rose, two drops of jasmine oil, and half a teaspoon of olive oil. Mix it all together and over your head it goes. Next, pick up the rose petals and place them inside a dry towel. Pat them dry, then place them under your pillow for the passionateevening you are desperately seeking.

31
MY FAMILY'S SPELLS ON THE GO

My family and I still do the quick fixes in this chapter when we're in need. My mother has so much information in that little stubborn head of hers that she always surprises me, and the energies here have proved their worth time and time again in our family's magical workings.

I know my Cuban heritage, and we Cubans tend to inflate problems. Conflicts and discord are fed to a frenzy, and guess what happens in my family next . . . well, immediately incense is burned, then out come the herbs, colored cloths, crystals, and candles. Then, to solve the problem, the scent of magic surrounds the room from years of know-how.

Now, in the meantime while all this is happening, my family has not stopped arguing and talking over each other. We are all trying to solve the particular problem that has suddenly arisen for one of the Abrev clan; it's like a war zone! We all want to protect the one who needs protection, and finally we come up with a sensible magical medium and the spell is written, to be done by the one who is in need. But even though we help create spells for each other, we never *do* those spells for the person in need; we each do our own spells, as it has more meaning when you actually get down and visualize your own needs to the universe.

The following few spells are all quick fixes that my family uses and has used with positive results over the years. They are simple and at times strange, but these quick spells have been tested over and over again and shared with others for a particular need. I'm sure you will find something in my family's spells on the go that you can use for your own needs.

MY FAMILY'S SPELLS ON THE GO
PROTECTION FROM NEGATIVE ENTITIES

When you feel a negative entity is nearby, get a glass of water and splash some cologne inside it. On top of the glass, place a pair of sharp scissors. Light some frankincense incense around your home and also light a white candle. Then, when you are mentally ready, call out to the entity and say, "I'm cutting the energies you feed from and sending you into the light. You must leave me alone and go toward the light."

Spell intention: The water is used to purify the room. The splash of cologne attracts lost entities and acts as a calling note. The frankincense brings protection energies against the entity, and the white candle attracts what is good in them. This spell is best done on a Saturday.

OTHER QUICK SPELLS ON THE GO FOR PROTECTION FROM NEGATIVE ENTITIES:

Place a laurel leaf under your pillow for protection.

Sprinkle ammonia around the house.

Light frankincense or dragon's blood incense.

Light a black candle and a white candle together—the black
  for the negative entity to go away, and the white for it to go
  in peace and hope.

CLEANSING THE BODY
OF NEGATIVE ENERGY

On a Monday, take an egg from your refrigerator and let it sit
out all night under the moonlight. On Tuesday morning, go to
a place where you can have some privacy—your bathroom will
do—and take all your clothes off. Once you're naked, take the
egg in your right hand, or left if you are left-handed, and gently
rub the egg all over your body. As you do, visualize the negative
energy you wish to be rid of. Once you finish, take the egg and
break it over your toilet. Let the yolk and egg whites flush down
the toilet, and just throw the shell in the garbage can.

Spell intention: My family uses this method to rid ourselves of negative energy—negative energy that someone else
has created for us or simply energy that we have created for
ourselves.

As you rub the egg over your body, the egg absorbs all the
negativity from your body. By flushing the contents of the egg
down the toilet, you are flushing that negative energy as far away

as you can. The toilet is a means of getting rid of waste, and with this spell you are getting rid of your negative energy waste.

OTHER QUICK SPELLS ON THE GO
FOR CLEANSING THE BODY
OF NEGATIVE ENERGY

Have a salt bath, or do a bucket spell with salt.

Light a black candle and blue candle together, and wish the negative energy to go away.

Carry with you a tiger's-eye crystal.

FREEZE THOSE WHO DO US HARM

Fill a clear glass with water. Then, on a small piece of paper, write down the name of the person you know is doing you harm, and tarnishing your reputation, by means of gossip or anger. As you do this, visualize what you would like this person to stop doing, then place the paper with his or her name inside the glass of water. Add one drop of blue food dye, and with a small teaspoon stir together the paper and the food dye in the glass of water. Immediately place the mixture inside your freezer.

Spell intention: The water in the glass makes the connection with the name of the person, and then the blue dye cools off the person you want to stop. By placing the glass inside your freezer, you will freeze any negative intentions toward you.

This spell is one of my favorites, and it works every single time. Do not take this person out of the freezer until you feel his or her negativity has calmed down. If the negativity starts again, do the spell again—but this time add one peppercorn to the water, which will indicate that you mean business.

OTHER QUICK SPELLS ON THE GO FOR THOSE WHO WOULD DO US HARM

Light a red candle in the name of the one who is doing you harm, and visualize that person stopping it right *now*.

Carry with you a laurel leaf where no one can see it, or a few pine nuts.

MONEY

Carry with you phony paper currency—the higher the denomination, the better.

Spell intention: The universe is all about visualizing and staying positive. If you think negatively, you will bring nothing but negative energy, but the more you think in a positive way, the more good things you'll attract. This goes for money, too: the more you have, the more you'll get. Treat your phony paper currency as though it were real, and never, never give it away.

OTHER QUICK SPELLS
ON THE GO FOR MONEY

Light a green candle every Thursday.

Carry alfalfa inside your purse or wallet at all times.

Carry with you a cowry shell.

Place cinnamon sticks in a decorative bowl and add to the bowl a cup of sesame seeds. Use the bowl as a centerpiece on top of your dinning room table. Refresh it as needed, as long as your money needs last.

Get a large bunch of fresh basil and caress yourself with it from head to toe.

Write yourself a check and don't deposit it—but keep it with you at all times.

Fill a half-shell of a coconut with uncooked rice and place it behind your front door.

Place one drop of patchouli essential oil in your hands in order to take hold of your money needs.

PROTECTION FOR THE HOME

Find or purchase a clear or white spray bottle, although a blue spray bottle will also do. Once you've got your bottle, place inside it seven rusty nails, seven sewing pins, a tiger's-eye crystal, two large tablespoons of rum, and one drop of blue food dye.

Now add water to the bottle, preferably rainwater, and then add four drops of basil essential oil and two large sticks of fresh rosemary leaves. Mix all this together and leave it outside on a full-moon night. Keep the spray bottle and the mixture inside it outside for three more days and three more nights. Let the moon give the bottle its protection strength.

Next, spray the water inside the bottle all over your home on Saturdays to keep your home protected and to magically clean up the negative energy.

Spell intention: In this spell are many protection energies, and once they are mixed together you create a powerful protection liquid that, once it is left under the moonlight and sprayed in your home, will give your home a protection coating that no negativity will be able to penetrate.

OTHER SPELLS ON THE GO FOR THE PROTECTION OF YOUR HOME

Sprinkle ammonia around the house when needed for negativity.

Burn rosemary incense whenever possible to keep negativity away.

Hang a bunch of garlic from the front door.

Behind the front door, keep a red bow.

Place in the four corners of your home four clear quartz crystals, with each of the points facing toward the outside of your residence.

Light blue candles for protection on Tuesdays and Saturdays.

Mix together salt and aloe powder, and sprinkle it around your home.

Always have a clear quartz crystal around your home for protection.

OTHER FAMILY FAVORITES
PROTECTION FOR YOUR CHILDREN

Have your child wear an onyx or a tiger's-eye crystal.

Visualize a blue light around your child at all times.

Never let your child wear red—instead, he or she should wear
yellow or blue for protection.

TO HELP YOUR CHILD
AFTER A NIGHTMARE

Get your child a stuffed animal. It could be any animal your
child can identify with, such as a tiger, a lion, or a bear. If your
child has a bad nightmare, tell him or her to hold this stuffed
animal and to visualize the toy as a real animal that will protect
against that which has scared your child during the nightmare.

TO ATTRACT A MAN

Sew a little red bow on the back of all your underwear.

Have a bucket shower with rose petals.

Carry with you a rose-quartz crystal.

TO KEEP SOMEONE HAPPY
AND ON YOUR SIDE

Write the name of the person you wish to have on your side
and place the paper on a white plate. Then add honey on top
and place the plate up high, where it cannot be seen by any-

one. This spell can also be done for a person who needs some sweetening!

FOR STUDY, RESEARCH, OR CONCENTRATION

Light a yellow candle.

Burn rosemary oil in your oil burner.

Carry with you a citrine crystal.

TO THWART YOUR ENEMY

On a piece of toilet paper, write the name of the person who has been causing you harm. Flush the toilet paper down the toilet, and whatever your enemy was doing will stop. Now, if you'd like to be more creative with the toilet tissue, please be my guest!

CLOSING

Each living thing possesses an energy field, within and around it, that is filled with earthbound vibrations. When you combine those natural energies with positive thoughts, you generate your wishes and send them to the universe. In spells on the go, you do just that—but without a ritual, so you're able to keep up with the fast pace of modern life.

The more you visualize your needs to the universe, the more the spell will go your way. But if it doesn't, don't despair. There is always a reason, and soon enough you will find out why.

Thank you for letting me share my family's spells and my spells with you. Enjoy them, as they have proved to be very handy in my times of need.

Blessed be,
Ileana

AFTERWORD

These spells are for individual growth and evolution. We don't
want to infringe on others, assume we know what others desire, or want anyone else to be other than who they are. The
spells work best when we wish for change in ourselves. We can
then become healthier, happier, and more abundant, radiating
a light that will in turn attract what we want in life. Remember, we already hold the greatest power to our own evolution;
when we visualize what we want, it does appear.

SPELL
WORKSHEETS

You can create your own spell book (also known as a Book of Shadows) by purchasing a blank notebook and writing out the same questions from the following pages.

SPELL WORKSHEET

Date spell conducted:

Reason for conducting the spell:

The way you were feeling before the spell:

The way you were feeling after the spell:

Time it took for the spell to manifest:

Noticeable changes made by the spell:

SPELL WORKSHEET

Date spell conducted:

Reason for conducting the spell:

The way you were feeling before the spell:

The way you were feeling after the spell:

Time it took for the spell to manifest:

Noticeable changes made by the spell:

GLOSSARIES

GLOSSARY FOR WHITE SPELLS

Altar: A sacred place created for magical workings.

Altar candles: Two candles placed on an altar to represent the day of the week.

Amulet: A charm or ornament used for protection or for an intent.

Astral candle: A candle of the color associated with an individual's astrological sign.

Astral realm: A parallel universe that is not physical but a mirror image of ourselves and the things around us.

Astral travel: Separation from the self; an out-of-body experience where you are aware of what is around you.

Aura: Invisible colors that radiate outside a physical form.

Censer: A small container used for burning incense.

Charcoal tablet: A special kind of charcoal that when lit can be used to burn dried herbs.

Cleansing crystals: Purifying crystals using natural energies. For example, salt and water prepare crystals for individual needs.

Dressing candles: A ritual conducted to ready candles for an intent.

Guide: A spiritual guide or guardian angel.

Herb: A plant—annual, biennial, or perennial—that dies back each year. There are aromatic, culinary, and medicinal herbs.

Karma: The law of the universe that keeps the balance of right and wrong.

Lucumí: An African-based religion now being practiced in Puerto Rico and Cuba. Better known as *Santería*.

Magic: The use of natural energies and positive visualization to create change in our lives.

Magical baths: Baths that are taken with natural energies to manifest dreams, to relieve stress, and to establish a connection with the water element.

Mind's eye: Used to see visualizations in one's mind as if they were movie clips.

Mother Earth: The spirit of the planet Earth.

North Pole: A name given to the top of a candle, from the center to the wick.

Oil burner: A deep ceramic dish with a tea candle on the bottom used for burning essential oil.

Parchment paper: Originally, a paper that was made out of animal skin. Today, imitations may be purchased from office supply outlets.

Ritual: The act of preparing the spiritual self by gathering magical tools and conducting magical workings or any type of religious act.

Santería: A magical practice that originated in Africa.

Santero: A competent herbalist and spiritual adviser in the Lucumí tradition.

Snuffer: A tool used to extinguish candles.

South Pole: A name given to the bottom of a candle, from the center down.

Spell: A combination of focusing on your needs while using positive thought patterns and some of nature's natural energies.

Third eye: Known as the sixth chakra, located in the middle of the brow. The third eye is the center of our creative perception which works with our subconscious mind to enhance psychic abilities.

Visualization: The art of concentration used for seeing and making things happen.

White spell: Any spell conducted for a positive outcome that does not use the manipulation of others.

GLOSSARY FOR
WHITE SPELLS FOR LOVE

Abyss: A dark place that unconsciously feeds our depression or negative state of mind.

Affirmation: A positive statement one makes about oneself or a situation.

Aura field: The field that surrounds all of us, the colors that radiate outside our physical bodies.

Dark love: Manipulating love for one's own selfish needs.

Broken heart: The intense feeling of loss after the end of a relationship.

Chakras: The seven light points of our bodies.

Charcoal tablets: Carbon used to burn incense.

Crystals: Semiprecious stones used to promote health, happiness, luck, and spirituality if carried or used with intent.

Essential oils: Oils extracted from flowers, plants, or resins.

Etheric field: The field of pure energy that radiates outside our physical bodies.

Human nature: Behavior of people resulting from their culture, attitudes, or values.

Karma: The law of the universe: "what goes around, comes around."

The Love Box: A box in which we keep all that we need to conduct a love spell.

Magic: The use of natural energies and positive visualization to create change in our lives.

Magical supplier/New Age store: A shop that sells ingredients and equipment necessary for magical spells.

Manipulative love: Forcing the love of another when it doesn't exist.

Positive visualization: Remaining positive while visualizing your needs to both the universe and yourself.

Romantic love: The love we share when we are in a romantic relationship

Self-love: The love you feel for yourself when you accept who you are.

The "tools": Items and ingredients necessary for conducting spells.

GLOSSARY FOR WHITE SPELLS
FOR PROTECTION

Altar: A sacred place created for magical workings.

Astral colors: Colors of the astrological star signs.

Astral projection: Separation from the self, an out-of-body experience during which one is aware.

Aura field: The field that surrounds all of us, the colors that radiate outside our physical bodies.

Bad spirits: Earth-bound entities who have not crossed over, some of whom think they are still alive; they often do work for dark forces in return for something promised for the bad spirits' services.

Chain letter: A letter that attempts to manipulate and threaten the recipients with bad luck if the instructions in the chain letter are not followed exactly.

Chakras: The seven light points of our bodies.

Crystals: Semi-precious stones used to promote health, happiness, luck, and spirituality if carried or used with intent.

Curses: Thought patterns aimed, with destructive intent, at an individual due to the insecurities, jealousy, or anger of the one doing the curse.

Curses within: Curses people bring on themselves due to their own negative thinking.

Dark occult forces: People who practice magic obscurely and negatively.

Death card: One of the major arcana cards of the tarot, it represents change and the death of something old that will bring something new.

Defense magic: The form of magic used to defend ourselves from those who wish us harm.

Essential oils: Oils extracted from flowers, plants, or resins.

Higher realm: A higher plane of existence, a parallel universe that is not physical.

Human nature: Behavior of people resulting from culture, attitudes, or values.

Magic: The use of natural energies and positive visualization to create change in our lives.

Negative magic and negative workings: The use of natural energies and negative visualization to create change in others' lives without their awareness.

Pentagram: Five-pointed star used by Wiccans and Pagans. The pentagram represents the elements and the realm between the spirit and the human body.

Perpetual curses: Curses inflicted by those who are closest to you and words and violence used to destroy a person emotionally and spiritually.

Protection: The guarding of a person and his or her loved ones against another's wrongdoings.

Unforgiven curses: Curses that continue through many different lifetimes.

Universal law: The law of karma: "What goes around, comes around."

Vampires of light: Individuals who lack self-esteem and therefore feed from yours. They leave you feeling totally exhausted though they themselves feel better when they are with you.

GLOSSARY FOR
WHITE SPELLS ON THE GO

Astral travel: Separation from the self, an out-of-body experience during which one is aware.

Chakras: The seven light points, and life forces, in our bodies.

Charcoal tablets: A special kind of charcoal that, when lit, can be used to burn herbs and resins.

Dressing a candle: Anointing a candle with specific oils for a particular intent.

Earthbound energies: Energies with life, such as herbs, plants, and crystals.

Essential oils: Oils extracted from flowers, plants, or resins.

Etheric field: The field of pure energy that radiates outside our physical bodies.

Herb: A plant that is valued for its medicinal properties or for its flavor. There are aromatic, culinary, and medicinal herbs.

Magic: The use of natural energies and positive visualization to create change in our lives.

Magical workings: The act of doing and using magic.

New Age store: A shop that sells everything you need for magic, including herbs, crystals, candles, and self-help books that teach spirituality.

Oil burner: A deep, sometimes ceramic, dish with a tea candle on the bottom that is used for burning essential oils.

Santería: A magical practice that originated in Africa.

Talisman: Anything that wards away negative energies and entities.

TO WRITE TO THE AUTHOR

If you wish to contact the author or would like more information about this book, please write to the author in care of Llewellyn Worldwide Ltd. and we will forward your request. Both the author and publisher appreciate hearing from you and learning of your enjoyment of this book and how it has helped you. Llewellyn Worldwide Ltd. cannot guarantee that every letter written to the author can be answered, but all will be forwarded. Please write to:

Ileana Abrev
⅏ Llewellyn Worldwide
2143 Wooddale Drive
Woodbury, MN 55125-2989

Please enclose a self-addressed stamped envelope for reply, or $1.00 to cover costs. If outside the U.S.A., enclose an international postal reply coupon.

Many of Llewellyn's authors have websites with additional information and resources. For more information, please visit our website at http://www.llewellyn.com